A HARROWSMITH GARDENER'S GUIDE

ROCK GARDENS

EDITED BY KATHARINE FERGUSON

ILLUSTRATIONS BY MARTA SCYTHES

CAMDEN HOUSE

CAMDEN
•HOUSE•
♦♦♦♦♦♦
PUBLISHING

© Copyright 1988 by Camden House
Publishing

Canadian Cataloguing in Publication Data

Main entry under title:

Rock Gardens

(Harrowsmith gardener's guides)
Includes index
ISBN 0-920656-90-0

1. Rock gardens. I. Ferguson, Katharine. II Series.

SB459.R62 1988   635.9'672   C88-093789-0

Trade distribution by
Firefly Books
3520 Pharmacy Avenue, Unit 1-C
Scarborough, Ontario
Canada M1W 2T8

Printed in Canada for
Camden House Publishing Ltd.
(a division of Telemedia Publishing Inc.)
7 Queen Victoria Road
Camden East, Ontario
K0K 1J0

Design by
Linda J. Menyes

Cover by
Jonathan Milne

Colour separations by
Herzig Somerville Limited
Toronto, Ontario

Printed and bound in Canada by
D.W. Friesen & Sons
Altona, Manitoba

Acknowledgements

The Harrowsmith Gardener's Guide to Rock Gardens took shape through the enthusiasm and cooperation of a great many people. They include art director Linda Menyes; artist Marta Scythes, who prepared the botanical sketches; senior editor Jennifer Bennett; assistant editors Jill Walker and David Archibald; typesetter Patricia Denard-Hinch; production manager Susan Dickinson; graphic artist Susan Gilmour; copy editors and associates Sara Perks, Charlotte DuChene, Mary Patton, Cathy De Lury, Christine Kulyk, Bob Weisnagel, Geri Savits-Fine, Peggy Denard; associate publisher Frank Edwards; associate editor Tracy C. Read; assistant editor Merilyn Mohr; and Adèle Crowder, curator of the Queen's University Herbarium. Appreciation must also be expressed to those who made accessible their rock gardens and/or their special expertise: Cy and Molly Baker, Gordon and Jean McGibbon, Terry Leduc, Andrew Osyany, and Harold Crawford.

The quotations at the head of each chapter are from *A Book About The Garden* (Thomas Nelson & Sons; London, 1892) by S. Reynolds Hole, dean of Rochester cathedral, England.

Contents

Chapter One:
A Brief History of Rock Gardens

By Jennifer Bennett

"N o gardener . . . has made experiments, however small, in the formation of a rock garden and in the culture of alpine plants without bringing a new gladness to himself and others." ✐ Although most modern rock gardens are either conservative stone walls or quiet areas of limestone interplanted with delicate alpines, rock gardens of the past have been far more remarkable. True, some spots were subtle and lovely enough to inspire today's best matchmaking of stone and plant. But others varied from the ugly to the bizarre to the almost impossibly spectacular. ✐ The ancestry of every backyard collection of granite boulders and sempervivums, for instance, includes monoliths that attempted to duplicate the grandeur of real mountain ranges. The pinnacle of this type of early 19th-century garden was reached by a structure that laid claim to a corner of an English private estate. Called "Mer de Glace" and "Alps at Chamonix," Lady Broughton's substantial rockwork towered to three or four times the height of a person and mimicked the real French Alps with its own rugged peaks, valleys, trees, wildflowers and simulated glaciers made of grey limestone, quartz and spar, the interstices filled with white marble to give the impression of snow. By mid-century, the small mountains even featured beehives shaped like Swiss chalets. Garden writer Jane Loudon wrote that 7 the garden demanded of her contemporary Lady Broughton "a great deal of her time for six or eight years," and still, "it was a task of greatest difficulty to make it stand against the weather." Perhaps "gladness" was not Lady Broughton's only response to the intricate project she had taken on.

This sort of grand endeavour, considered more admirable than eccentric in a romantic age, was the offspring of even stranger rock gardens of previous centuries: Stonehenge-like ruins and damp grottoes studded with shells. These, too, could be considered early rock gardens, because even though alpine plants were likely to be overwhelmed here—impact was stressed more than environment—much was being learned about plants and their requirements. Often young evergreens were planted for effect, but they soon dwarfed the rest of the panorama. Climbers and ground covers were apt to smother rocks, grottoes, glaciers and less aggressive plants alike. If the alpines faded and died, the gardener knew that something more than spectacle was needed to sustain them. The foundations of today's rock gardens consist of centuries of such experiments.

By 1890, the garden of English millionaire Frank Crisp featured 7,000 tons of rocks, some as heavy as 6½ tons apiece, forming a miniature Matterhorn surrounded by simulated snowfields. A second garden at the same site, accessible only through artificial caves and grottoes, consisted entirely of concrete "rocks." Less wealthy gardeners copied the style as well as they could, decorating piles of rubble with miniature cast-iron mountain goats and chalets.

Some of these early rock gardens could be, and often were, more accurately called rockworks, stoneries or rockeries. Collections of all types of natural objects, from pressed flowers to shells, had been the rage for a century, and rockeries were, of course, perfect places for displaying various geological objects as well as an assortment of other weatherproof things. "Rarities and curiosities," wrote John Loudon in his encyclopaedia of 1859, "are occasionally introduced in gardening, such as the jawbones of the whale, basaltic columns, lava blocks, pillars of earthy rock salt. The tufa, corals and madrepores brought from Otaheite by Captain Cook as ballast, now form part of the rockwork in the Chelsea garden." That rockwork also displayed flints, chalk, fossils, lava from Iceland and stones from the Tower of London. Another rockery, according to a 19th-century author, shone with red coral, "the bright vermilion of which eclipses the hue of all the Phloxes and Mesembryanthemums that can be made to grow" on its surface.

Richardson Wright, a noted garden writer of the 1930s, observed of such gardens: "The stones assumed greater importance than the plants that grew between them. In fact, any incidental plant capable of holding its height down to less than a foot found a home among these rocks and gave delight to boastful gardeners." Rock gardener Reginald Farrer added scornfully: "In some dark corner or in some dank, tree-haunted hollow, you rigged up a dump of broken cement blocks and added bits of stone and fragments of statuary. You called this 'the Rockery' and proudly led your friends to see it and planted it all over with periwinkle to hide the hollows in which your Alpines had promptly died. In other words, you considered only the stones and not the plants that were to live among them. No wonder, then, that the rockery came soon to be looked on as the rich man's extravagant fad."

Not until the end of the 19th century was there a real interest in alpine plants for their own sake. Although Lady Broughton's rockwork did have some alpine plants described by an observer as "rare and beautiful," they played only the smallest of supporting roles—no greater

Not until the 19th and 20th centuries was there a popular European interest in such subtle rock garden candidates as certain small North American asters.

than the beehives—in the overall panorama. Alpine plants, which usually flower for just a short period each year, are tough in their own environment, where they endure wind, heat, drought, snow and extreme cold, but they demand certain conditions that can be best supplied in a rocky situation: well-drained soil, exposure to the open air, crevices, sometimes even a sloped surface. Gathered in the wild and brought to lower altitudes where their owners knew little or nothing about their requirements, they had a reputation for being difficult to grow. It was not until 1864, when Austrian botanist Kerner von Merilaun collected alpines from his native mountains and attempted to grow them in the lowlands at the Royal Botanical Gardens in Innsbruck, that it was demonstrated they could be cultivated in quantity with any great success at all. Von Merilaun constructed a garden on a slope covered with

stones "to represent in miniature the valleys of the Tyrolese Alps," according to Reginald Farrer. This was, in contrast with the earlier peaks and cliffs, an artificial scree or moraine, a type of rock garden that would become increasingly popular. Von Merilaun's scree turned out to be an extremely successful example of what was then known as an alpinum, a display of different mountain plants.

Among the thousands of new plant species introduced to Europe during the 18th and 19th centuries (when every important expedition included its own botanist or naturalist) came a certain small proportion of alpines and meadow wildflowers. But the interest in these subtle, difficult flowers never matched the mania for showy tropicals, so it was not until the late 19th and early 20th centuries that many alpines were introduced in Europe. William Robinson's *Alpine Flowers for Gardens* (1871) was the first book entirely 9 devoted to the subject. Stories of the alpine-seeking botanists from this era are often compelling, depicting both the social contexts and the natural environments of the wildflowers. In his article "Two Days Hunting on the Screes," published in *The Scree Garden* (1933), H. Roger-Smith writes: "My friend Mr. W.E. Th. Ingwersen and I spent the night in the hayloft of the Baraché Inn and, after an early bathe in the stream and a frugal breakfast of coffee and black bread, climbed to the top of the mountain. As we reached the crest, we saw the rocks in every direction red with the flowers of *Primula wulfeniana*; they were in incredible numbers, and the effect was most beautiful."

Still, if homemade mountain ranges were no longer in fashion and alpine plants were increasingly available, gardeners continued to be unsure about just what a rock garden should be. Among the more successful gardens were those created by James Pulham, who became well known for the creation of a type of concrete known as Pulhamite and who believed that "it is all very well, pleasing and interesting to grow the pretty little Alpines and Ferns, and it is in the screes or debris at the base of the cliff that they will do well and will be seen best; but for the rugged and bold picturesque effect or grandeur, we must have the noble cliff, if only as high as our heads." Pulham and Son built the Royal Horticultural Society's rock garden at Wisley, which consisted of terraces that descended an embankment. In another style, rock gardens were excavated rather than built and the resulting cliffs planted, sometimes spectacularly, with trees and vines. Not all efforts worked as well. Reginald Farrer, who himself built a moraine in Clapham, which he described in *My Rock Garden* (1907), called many of his contemporaries' efforts "almond puddings," "dog's graves" or "Devil's lapfuls," of which "the chaotic hideousness of the result is to be remembered with shudders ever after." Farrer

As Gertrude Jekyll noted, "The right way is also the most beautiful way."

added that the word "natural . . . has deluded so many into thinking that . . . you just drop the stones all over the place and it comes right."

Even by 1929, eminent American botanist L.H. Bailey was complaining that "many of the so-called rock gardens are mere heaps of stones, placed where it seems to be convenient to pile stones rather than where the stones may improve conditions for the growing of plants." Bailey noted conclusively, "If one is making a collection of rocks, he is pursuing geology rather than gardening."

It was in part thanks to Farrer's contributions that home gardeners came to understand what made a good rock garden: rocks and plants in pleasing proportions, so that the entire area appeared unified and natural with neither plants nor stones overwhelming the effect. Richardson Wright wrote in his introduction to Louise Beebe Wilder's *Pleasures and Problems of a Rock Garden* (1937) that the change came about when the emphasis shifted from rocks to alpine plants. "Immediately, a new vitality seized the movement . . . . Rock gardens were to be made for rock plants, not for stones. The rock garden should reproduce *in parvo* the environment in which these mountain plants naturally grew. Geology was dethroned, and ecology assumed its place. Not until this came to pass did rock gardening deserve serious consideration."

Recently, the Chinese and Japanese traditions of rock gardening have influenced Western landscaping. Best known are the Japanese dry gardens created by Zen monks since the 15th century. Here, stones may simulate landscapes in miniature, but their main role is to lead the mind of the viewer to peaceful contemplation. In quite a different way, Chinese gardeners have used rocks not only in collections, to build mounts and grottoes, but also alone, in place of statuary. Most prized are the pitted and convoluted rocks taken from the bottom of Lake Tai Hu and often regarded as objets d'art. According to the *Yuan Yeh* (1635), these stones "may be placed under a stately pine or be combined with wonderful flowers. They may be used as mountains set up in a big pavilion out in the garden . . . . They have been collected since time immemorial." Twelfth-century artist Mi Fei so respected one of his stones that he called it his "elder brother," while the modern writer Chuin Tung wrote that "when stone is endowed with personality, one can find it delightful company."

While both of these traditions have tended to make Westerners more aware of the importance of selecting just the right stones for just the right situations, the idea of a rock garden as a place primarily designed to display plants in a pleasing, authentic environment remains the dominant one in the West. "Today," wrote Richardson Wright, "one cannot boast that she has a complete garden unless it contains at least a few of the representative alpines set in their proper environment."

Perhaps the last word should rightfully go to Gertrude Jekyll, a famous English landscape designer who wrote, in *Wall and Water Gardens* (1901): "If any success in the cultivation of rock plants is expected, it is only reasonable to suppose that one must take the trouble to learn something about the plants, their kinds and their needs, and it is equally necessary

Among the recent influences on Western rock gardens are Japanese dry gardens.

to take the trouble to learn how their places are to be prepared. Happily for the chances of success and pleasure in this delightful kind of gardening, the right way is also the most beautiful way."

Cause for "a new gladness," indeed.

Jennifer Bennett is senior editor of *Harrowsmith* magazine, editor of *A Harrowsmith Gardener's Guide to Ground Covers* and *The Harrowsmith Landscaping Handbook*, and author of the *Harrowsmith Northern Gardener*.

Chapter Two:
Stone and Sand and Peat

By Pat J. Tucker

“Of course, when I speak of a gardener, I mean a man who uses his eyes and his ears . . . who does not select a clay soil for flowers which repose in sand or a shady place for those which only thrive in sunshine; does not set a giant amid dwarfs and allow him to overpower them all, but thinks beforehand and watches always. To such a man, the introduction of the alpine garden . . . is a new and large delight . . . and yet you rarely find them even where there is the very spot for a rock garden and stone and sand and peat are at hand.” ◌ My introduction to the alpine garden occurred on the thin, acidic soils of North Devon, where my mother had created a garden in the local shale and where, as they used to say, "it rains six days out of seven, and on the seventh day, it pours." Despite the muddy difficulties of such a location, I loved rock gardening, the association of stone and plant that is a unique juxtaposition of the strong and the delicate, the permanent and the ephemeral. In the sixties, after a move to Canada, I was able to put my Wellington boots aside, although my enthusiasm for rock gardening continued. My reeducation began in relatively dry southwestern Ontario and continued on the alkaline clay soils of the Guelph region, not far from Toronto. ◌ Regardless of regional geographic and climatic disparities, there are certain principles of 13 rock gardening that remain constant. All rock gardens require some amount of exposure to the light, as well as aerated soil with excellent drainage. The basic rules for creating a beautiful, sturdy framework are the same everywhere, although, of course, aesthetics vary from gardener to gardener and situation to situation. Rock gardens may be informal or natural, imitating the cliffs, rock slides, screes and moraines of nature – a few fortunate gardeners have their own outcrops, which can be used to make excellent gardens – or they may entail formal structures, such as rock walls or patios, which are very much man-made but no less attractive because of it.

My reeducation in Canada began with the creation of three rock gardens, each one quite different from the others. The first small effort was located next to the house foundation, facing west and partially shaded by trees. Exposed daily to six hours of sun and amply covered with snow in winter, it made a perfect home for fall-flowering gentians. Later, I extended a portion to the north. This had only three hours' exposure to the sun, and here, spring gentians flourished. My second garden was built into a long bank that divided an upper lawn from a vegetable garden some six feet below. Oriented to the southwest, it received long hours of sunshine and so was suited to alpines that tolerate drier conditions. My present rock garden is rather unique, since it belongs in part to my neighbour to the south. Built between our properties on a common slope that drops 8 feet in 30 (a 25 percent grade), it is oriented, again, toward the southwest. Since the houses are only 12 feet apart and his house thus shades the garden, two distinct microclimates occur. My side receives morning sun and is planted with more difficult-to-grow plants, while my neighbour's portion receives full afternoon sun and so can accommodate more drought-resistant species. An environmental factor here,

Informal, or natural, rock gardens imitate the forms and patterns of nature.

beloved by the alpine plants, is a constant gentle breeze produced by the proximity of the two houses.

Site Selection

I have had to make use of both flat and sloping sites, small and large, offering different amounts of exposure to the sun. In choosing a site for a proposed rock garden, the designer must deal with such limitations and must also take into account other garden areas planned or already present, the architecture of the house and whether or not there are outcrops that can be utilized. In general, an informal, or natural, rock garden is appropriate to an area some distance from the house, while a more formal garden works better in association with the house itself. Some would add that any sort of rock garden – except a natural outcrop – is out of place on the front lawn. But none of these are hard-and-fast rules. Only the prospective rock garden owner can assess the potential of his or her own land and determine the overall picture within which the rock garden will lie.

Consider not only the site itself but also how it may be seen from the house windows or other vantage points, how it may be approached or framed – perhaps by a few tall evergreens behind, small shrubs or trees to the side – and how it will be oriented, ideally to the east or southeast so that plants will have some respite from the summer sun and heat. On most urban properties, the choice of site is limited. Nevertheless, slopes and undulations can be utilized in even the smallest area to create a very attractive outcrop. Close to the house, sloping ground may be transformed by a rock wall and terrace. Or if the plot is completely flat, there is always the option of putting in raised beds, planting within and around a flagstone patio or using troughs and other containers. All of these are elements of a more formal approach, often planned as extensions of the house itself.

Rural gardeners have a far greater choice of site. For instance, a rock garden could merge with or grow out of a wild garden, allowing woodland and alpine species to make a nodding acquaintance. Just make sure it has adequate sun and is not situated over tree or shrub roots, which can be highly competitive and require root-pruning every year. Alternatively, bury a foot-wide metal strip between the garden and the invasive roots – a more permanent solution. If rock is plentiful, plan a variety of areas from the informal to the most formal. (Rock work can become a magnificent obsession.) In all cases, be sure there is access to the site so that materials and equipment will cause as little damage as possible to established parts of the landscape.

When choosing a site, always consider the requirements of the plants. In addition to easy-care dwarfs such as moss pinks

(*Phlox subulata*), which are natives of North American lowlands, most gardeners will be aiming to grow some alpines and other plants from different environments. These may have specific needs for wind and sun that should be known ahead of time.

Rock Music

After site selection, the next step – unless, again, one is working with an existing outcrop – is choosing the rock. Most important, a well-orchestrated rock garden should be beautiful even before it is planted; the rocks and their situation must, in themselves, be satisfying to the

Stratified rocks should be arranged so that the lines are parallel.

beholder. For the informal garden, there are a few additional basic rules concerning rock selection:
• Use only one kind of rock;
• Use local rock if it is suitable;
• Avoid laying down cut stone or quarried blocks (which can be saved for a formal structure);
• Understand the difference between stratified and unstratified rock, because the whole nature of the garden and the way the rocks will be situated depend upon this distinction. 15

Any steep bank or abrupt change in grade provides an ideal location for the construction of a dry-stone wall, which can be built from quarried slabs.

Stratified rocks such as limestone and sandstone are sedimentary – that is, deposited gradually by water, layer by layer. Formed aeons ago in lakes and streambeds, these rocks show distinct parallel lines. Look at them in nature and observe how the lines follow through from one area of outcrop to the next. The Rocky Mountains are almost entirely formed of sedimentary rock, which can be seen ascending layer upon layer to the tops of the highest peaks. It is relatively easy to create a good-looking natural rock setting with limestone or sandstone; the latter has the advantage of a porous nature amenable to the root systems of many alpines searching for moisture and coolness.

Unstratified rocks may be igneous (formed by heat), such as granite and basalt; metamorphic, such as conglomerate; or man-made, such as concrete. These do not have distinct layers but do possess their own unique textures and colours. In a rock garden, they may be used to simulate glacial till, the rock and debris churned up by glaciers and deposited as the ice melted. This may take the form of groups of rounded, weathered rocks of varying sizes and shapes, surrounded and joined together by areas of smaller broken and cracked stones. Weather-worn, lichen-covered granite boulders are beautiful and, though more difficult than sedimentary rocks to combine in a way reminiscent of their natural random groupings, can still create a successful rock garden environment in the right hands.

Suitable rocks are available from several places. The best ones for the environment are those gathered from the garden site itself; they are also free of charge and in need of little transportation. A wheelbarrow and a strong constitution – remember to bend the knees, not the back – may be all you need. Local quarries and building sites are additional possible sources, although a farmer whose property abounds with rock would probably be quite happy, if surprised, to oblige you. If all else fails, garden centres sell lightweight rocks such as tufa and pumice, which are expensive and so best suited to small sites. Look carefully at the rocks and choose aesthetically pleasing pieces, preferably with some weathering, at least on the side that will be outermost. To assess the amount of rock you will need, figure out the surface area of the garden-to-be, and for a naturalistic garden, estimate that 10 to 40 percent should be exposed rock. For a formal structure such as a wall, patio or path, larger quantities are required; the appropriate amount may be ascertained by taking some measurements at the rock site, while keeping in mind the dimensions of the desired structure.

Whatever form the rock garden takes, excavation and preparation below ground level will be necessary. Once you have established the shape of the garden area, cut out the turf and dig up any remaining topsoil, piling it nearby for future use in the rock garden or elsewhere. Next, excavate to a depth of about a foot. If you are working into a slope, grade the subsoil into the terraces or contours the garden will take. Lay down 4 to 8 inches of clinker, rubble or coarse stones, and top that with 1 or 2 inches of coarse (¾-inch) gravel. These two layers may not be necessary if the subsoil is very coarse, sloping and naturally well drained, in which case simply digging in coarse sand or pea gravel may suffice. On the firm bed thus established, set the stones and infill the soil as you progress.

The Soil

Not just any soil will suffice, however. Topsoil that grows broccoli to perfection is not likely to be the best medium for a rock garden. Clay soil is death to rock plants; if this is what you have excavated, use it elsewhere. Also, weeds such as twitch grass and bindweed will compete most unfairly with slow-growing alpines. Get rid of them at the outset, either by fallowing the site for a few weeks and digging them out piece by piece or, alternatively – if reluctantly – by treating them with a systemic herbicide according to the manufacturer's instructions. Thereafter, weed seeds of other sorts will still germinate, of course, and their control will become part of the routine maintenance of the garden.

Alpines grow best in thin, weed-free soils full of rock shards, gravel and coarse material, which keep the soil well aerated and allow it to drain quickly; and if the soil is also interspersed with organic matter, it retains necessary moisture. One way to provide this requisite blend of aeration and water retention is to prepare your own mixture. An excellent one consists of equal parts good garden loam, sand, gravel and either compost or peat moss, mixed together and left in a tidy pile beside the excavation for use as construction proceeds.

Another possible medium is spent greenhouse soil, not widely available but something that I used in my first garden. To make a similar mixture, combine equal parts peat moss, perlite and potting soil, and for alpines, add another part of pea gravel. Such a mixture is expensive, but because it is sterile, it is weed-free. I found that it required nothing but summer irrigation. In addition, the low nutrient value of the mix suited the minimal needs of most of my alpine plants.

In my second garden, I used the existing material, which was clay, and added a 6-inch layer of the greenhouse mix to the planting pockets. This worked initially, and weed control was no problem, but the poor drainage of the clay beneath caught up with me over the winter, and I lost many plants. Such mistakes at the outset are very difficult to correct later on. With these experiences in mind, I excavated the base soil entirely in my third garden and moved it into my perennial borders. Then I shovelled gravel into the subsoil and prepared a growing mix for the planting pockets.

While many of the species commonly grown in rock gardens are satisfied with the loamy-sandy-gravelly soil mix previously described, other species may have more exacting needs in terms of acidity or alkalinity, also known as the soil's pH. The pH scale, numbered 1 to 14, indicates acidity at its lower end, alkalinity at its

With its cool, reviving sounds, water is a natural complement to rock.

upper end; neutral soil is 7. Many plants can tolerate a middle range from 6 to 7.5, but certain acid-lovers demand 6 or less and certain lime-lovers 7.5 or greater. To establish a reference point at the outset, it is a good idea to have the pH of your soil tested. The local agricultural representative or state agricultural extension department can offer instructions for doing this. A less accurate way of measuring pH is to purchase a home soil-test kit, available from some garden nurseries and mail-order seed companies. Soil for special plant pockets can be made more alkaline by the addition of ground limestone or more acidic with the addition of peat moss or pine needles.

Creating the Natural Garden

In designing a garden, some gardeners like to get their ideas down on paper, while others prefer to work directly on the ground, letting the garden evolve gradually. In both cases, there are a few rules to be observed:
•Start with a firm base (the drainage layer should provide this);
•Ensure that all rocks are completely stable;

•Work from the bottom, placing each stone on its broadest base and tilting it slightly toward the slope so that rainwater will trickle inward to plant roots;
•Bury ⅓ to ½ of each rock;
•Fill in soil firmly and completely, leaving no air pockets for unsuspecting roots to find later on. Work with the soil only when it is comparatively dry so that it does not become compacted.

If there is an existing outcrop or clump of boulders, the garden design is already established, at least in part. The rock area may make a perfect starting point, needing only to be thoroughly cleared of grass and weeds and replenished with the soil mix. More likely, there will be difficulties, such as no deep crevices for planting pockets. Plan for shallow-rooted species here, or let the rock remain bare and concentrate your efforts on the other areas. You could also move the rock around, if it is portable, until a satisfactory picture begins to appear. As you go, closely fill in the earth between and behind the rocks, planning for a depth of more than a foot of soil for planting.

Generally speaking, relatively more rock will be required on a steep slope than on a gentler one. In working with stratified rock, keep in mind that it is revealed in nature through erosion by water and wind, and aim to capture that effect. Remember that the lines of stratification should be as closely aligned as possible; the rock should look as though it is all joined in one formation beneath the ground. What may emerge is a terracelike structure, which is fine if that is what you want, but varying the heights of the stones throughout the garden structure can create a more dynamic effect. If steps form part of the plan, set the slabs well back into the earth for stability and keep the strata lines of the rock horizontal. If the garden is to have a winding pathway between two banked or sloping areas, provide particularly deep drainage under the path to carry away water that will run

Bury up to half the rock in soil to create a completely firm foundation.

off both sides during sudden downpours or after prolonged wet weather. The path can be built of rocks or irregular stepping-stones set firmly into sand and interplanted with ground covers or dwarf carpeting plants such as mother-of-thyme (*Thymus serpyllum*). If the garden is large enough, side paths may be added so that as many plants as possible can be seen and tended without one's having to climb over the stones.

In working with unstratified boulders, try to give the impression of an area deposited on a slope by receding glaciers, then weathered over centuries into a rounded mass. Whereas stratified rocks should appear to emerge from the soil by erosion, unstratified ones should look as though they have been imbedded forever. A few groupings of different-sized boulders with an occasional individual on its own are much more effective than rocks strewn at random over a slope. Bed them in deeply and firmly, at least to their widest circumference, and set them at a slight diagonal to the slope so that their "backs" are turned to it, their "faces" looking down and across it. Small hummocks and hollows created in setting the stones this way will add to the interest and variety of the garden. One or two of the rocks may be split, once they are set, to produce the niches or crevices which plants love and which do not occur as readily in granite as they do in stratified rock. Depending upon its size and strength, a rock can be split with anything from a hammer to another stone to a wood-splitting maul.

Creating the Formal Garden

It is perhaps not too farfetched to look at the elements of the formal rock garden as a theme and its variations. The theme is the dry-stone wall, while its variations are the many forms such a construction can spawn: terraces, dividing walls or raised beds. Even a patio of flagstones interspersed with creepers or tiny tuffets may be seen as a rock wall reduced to two dimensions.

Any steep bank or abrupt change in grade is ideal for the construction of a dry-stone wall; here, the cut fieldstone or quarried slabs unsuited to the informal garden come into their own. Use flat stones with at least one good square face.

Begin, as with the informal garden, by removing existing turf and topsoil from the structure area; dig down to the subsoil, and set the largest base stones into concrete or on 6 inches of compact gravel fill. The larger stones are set two deep for the base, followed by somewhat smaller 19 stones in successive layers on top. In areas where winters are very cold, a 4-inch drainage tile placed between the large base stones, extending the length of the wall and with an outlet at ground level, will help minimize problems of frost heaving. Each layer of rock is backfilled with the soil mixture previously described, instead of with mortar; behind the soil, a core of chipped stone within the wall will ensure good drainage.

As the wall progresses, lay down each level tipped very slightly inward to produce a slope – called a batter – of 10 to 15 degrees, or approximately 1 inch to 1 foot of wall height. This distributes the weight and allows water to trickle down the face

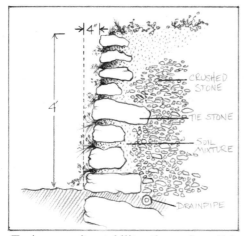

To increase its stability, the rock wall is created with a slight slope, called a batter.

of the wall and penetrate the plant pockets; it also gives the plants better exposure to sun. The wall should be no taller than 4 or 5 feet.

Ideally, plants are put in place during construction, their roots spread, covered and watered before the next course of stones is added. Usually, however, the plants are not available at that time, so small rocks can be inserted into the pockets to prevent soil erosion in the interim. The top of the wall can be infilled with soil for use as a planting bed, or it can

be finished with a layer of flat stones, or coping, which will create a more formal appearance.

One offshoot of the formal rock garden is trough gardening, so called because the idea first became popular when old stone water troughs were being discarded in the 1920s and 1930s. This type of alpine garden in miniature has a number of advantages. First, one can achieve variety in a small space and create a totally controlled artificial environment to suit the needs of fussy plants. Second, one can "rock garden" entirely without rocks or simply by adding one or two choice stones to enhance the planting. (The requirements of good drainage still apply, however; there should be at least 6 inches of coarse stone in the bottom of the trough.) While ready-made stone troughs are beautiful, they are seldom available outside of Europe and Britain. Alternatively, one can build an imaginative container using concrete, and a weathered, stony look is not too difficult to achieve.

Screes and Moraines

Scree is an accumulation of fragmented stone on a mountain slope or at the foot of a cliff. In the crevices, plants employ diverse survival techniques, including sending down long taproots. Scree drains thoroughly and quickly. A moraine is basically the same, at least as far as plants are concerned (although technically its fragments are the result of glacial action).

Imitations of scree sites and moraines provide the foundations for additional types of rock gardens. Usually, small areas within a rock garden are set aside to re-create the features of these natural formations, and here the most rock-oriented of all the plants may thrive as nowhere else. Many dry-land plants from the Rocky Mountains and elsewhere grow best in scree conditions, particularly if a top dressing of pea gravel is applied. This type of mulch, for instance, enhances

Because it is a confined space, a trough can be easily adapted to the needs of special or very small plants if soil, location and watering are adjusted.

the growth of such choice North American natives as *Lewisia cotyledon* and *L. rediviva.*

The scree must never be allowed to dry out and so needs frequent watering. Where the scree garden will be situated, excavate to the subsoil level, and infill with about a foot of rubble or coarse stone. The growing mixture should be well aerated and might consist of one part compost, one part sharp sand and three parts pea gravel. A moraine will require an underground watercourse – difficult or expensive to achieve for most home gardeners. Water does provide, however, a natural complement to rock, whether sliding beneath the surface of a moraine or trickling over glistening pebbles and dropping from pool to pool within a natural or formal garden, and rock garden enthusiasts may consider it a worthwhile feature, as I do. Even the murmur of water on a hot day is cooling and reviving; in some Oriental gardens, the sound of water is as important a feature as the visual elements.

Part of my first rock garden included a moraine that featured a concrete trough poured into the site and joined by an outlet to a small splash pool. About 6 inches of gravel was deposited in the trough, and atop that was the scree mixture of compost, sand and gravel. Water moved by gravity through the gravel into the splash pool and hence by a recycling pump back to the moraine inlet. Many choice alpines grew in this moraine, with its pump operating during hot, dry weather.

Such hot, dry periods seldom occurred in north Devon, where I was first acquainted with the delights of rock gardening. But then, most of the plants that inhabit rock gardens are native to neither England nor central Canada. These small plants, a harmonious group of former strangers brought together by gardeners in places as disparate as Devon and Ontario, are encouraged to grow far from their homelands and often in very different climates, with the simple tools of stone, sand and peat.

Pat Tucker, Head of Grounds and Vehicle Service Departments, University of Guelph, has recently launched Alpines Unlimited, which specializes in alpine plants and in the design and construction of rock gardens.

21

Chapter Three:
These Lovely Plants

By Marnie Flook

"Carefully prepared at the nurseries, or given by some friendly neighbour, placed with due regard to site and soil by those who have seen, heard or read of the habits of these lovely plants, their success is certain." ∽ The wall was a tapestry far more beautiful than anything I could have planned. Plants had formed shapely clumps or seeded themselves in crevices, or they had vanished unexpectedly, only to reappear in the terrace at the foot of the wall. Small green ferns also found a footing, and other little plants came unbidden. The pretty little candytuft, iberis, stayed neatly within its bounds. Sempervivum strung its succulent green beads along the rocks, and on top of the wall where they could be best enjoyed, the smallest, rarest treasures found their places – little jewels among the rough stones. Of all the rock gardens I have had, this wall has been the most permanent. Thirty-two years after I began it, it still looks attractive. ∽ Its beginning was not promising, however. That was in 1956, when I was a rock gardening novice faced with the challenge of planting a newly built stone wall and garden behind my family's home in Delaware. Some of the shrubs I planted threatened to take over the entire garden not long after, while other plants simply died. Nothing new had been written about rock gardening for years, and the old books I consulted were dis- 23

Dwarf conifers such as this juniper will not overwhelm the garden as they grow.

of the odd failing plant. I became committed to rock gardening and have remained so ever since.

Plant Choice

Rock gardens, I discovered, can be home not only to the low-growing perennial flowers one usually imagines but also to some well-chosen annual flowers and bulbs, miniature shrubs and dwarf conifers, small ferns and even a few ornamental grasses. And plants may come not only from mountainous regions but also from bogs, woodlands, seacoasts, heaths, prairies or arid plains – difficult environments where plants have had to struggle to survive wind, cold, poor soil, drought or shade and have adapted by developing interesting foliage and often large, beautiful flowers. Combining these different plants into a pleasing picture is the challenge of the rock gardener.

couraging. I was doing everything wrong. Rock garden plants, it seemed, were a special breed with particular needs and difficult habits. Then, luckily, I discovered several local nurseries whose owners were both optimistic and helpful, and during the next 10 years, four excellent books on rock gardening appeared (by Klaber, Schenk, Kolaga and Foster; see Resources). I joined the American Rock Garden Society, whose bulletins were full of descriptions of plants I hoped to grow and of gardens and mountain areas I hoped to visit. I read everything and was inspired to try again.

After removing the offending plants from the garden and adding sand and peat to the soil, I planted more appropriate varieties and finally mulched the garden with pebbles. This time, the rock garden thrived and needed very little maintenance save the removal of a few aggressive dwarf conifers and the replacement

This education is an ongoing process, learned in part from experience. When my husband and I moved from the country (and that first rock wall) to a city town house, we built planter boxes in the very small space available and planted four small rock gardens in them. This time, I used the right soil mix from the beginning and was careful to choose appropriate plants. Even so, I had a few disasters. Some plants that did well in the large wall garden did not thrive in the town house situation, and again, I made the mistake of planting a few dwarf conifers which grew too rapidly, although most of them have remained in scale. Each year, I still lose a few plants, but most have done well.

It is difficult to predict how plants will fare in varying situations, but the more knowledge one has at the outset, the better the chances for success. Read books, and join a rock garden society as I did. All offer their members a wealth of resources – garden tours, lectures, slide shows, newsletters full of challenging

Botanical gardens and rock garden societies introduce newcomers to suitable species such as the dramatic and sometimes challenging Lewisia rediviva.

ideas – and interaction with fellow gardeners. Visit botanical gardens and arboretums, attend plant shows or special exhibits, and poke around nurseries or garden centres, most of which display an array of rock garden plants. For real inspiration, get to know the plants in the wild, where you can see what they like – their preferred soil, exposure, climate and companion plants. Some of these elements can be reproduced at home.

The best rock garden plants have:
•Colourful, long-lasting flowers;
•Foliage that is attractive all year;
•A refined habit of growth;
•Hardiness in both winter and summer;
•A lack of special cultural needs.

Besides knowing the conditions in which plants will thrive, it is important to know their colour and time of bloom, as well as their habits of growth, so the plants can be combined in a satisfactory way. From early spring to late fall, some part of the garden should be in bloom. Consider foliage, also, when arranging plant palette combinations. What one wants to

Many of the familiar ground cover plants are so vigorous that they must be planted in situations where they will not dominate less invasive alpine varieties.

achieve is a blend of various colours and textures that will be pleasing whether or not the plants are in bloom.

The tiny mats, rosettes, cushions and clumps of the most prized plants should be situated close to eye level in a wall or raised bed or not too far from the paths, where they can be easily seen and protected from their more energetic neighbours. On the other hand, place plants with a spreading growth habit alongside each other or in walls or other areas where they will not overwhelm the smaller, choicer plants. These vigorous plants include many of the reliable, familiar rock garden plants usually available from garden centres, such as rock cress (*Arabis alpina*), aubrieta (*Aubrieta deltoidea*), moss pink (*Phlox subulata*), basket-of-gold (*Aurinia saxatilis*), evergreen candytuft (*Iberis sempervirens*), snow-in-summer (*Cerastium tomentosum*), soapwort (*Saponaria ocymoides*) and some of the larger forms of pinks (*Dianthus* spp) and bellflowers (*Campanula* spp).

It is usually best to start with plants that are easy to grow, species that have the greatest chance of being happy and establishing themselves permanently in your growing conditions. Then, let your plant repertoire grow along with your confidence. Eventually, most gardeners like to try their luck and skill with special plants they have admired or read about and coveted, even though they know they may be difficult.

Planting

The best time for planting is during mild weather, either in early spring before the heat of summer, when the ground is in good condition, or in early fall, when there is still time for the plants to become established before growth stops in winter. Mail-order plants should be ordered well enough in advance that they arrive four or five weeks before the actual planting, since they often have their roots wrapped in moss and are best treated as seedlings. Before putting them in the garden, pot them up in a sandy soil mixture until they are firmly rooted. Plants from local nurseries are already established and can go into the ground immediately. Place the conifers or shrubs first, then the rest of the plants. If the plants are in separate pots, move them around until you are satisfied with the arrangement. Even if you have drawn up a detailed plan in advance, you may find that you want to change it once you have the actual plants arranged in the garden.

In planting, dig a hole slightly larger than the root ball, carefully remove the plant from its container and place it in the hole, keeping the root ball as intact as possible. Be sure the plant is set at the same depth as it was in the pot, and fill in around the roots with more soil, pressing gently to firm the plant in place. If the plant has been in the pot for a long time, its roots may have formed a solid mass. In general, herbaceous perennial plants – those that die back to the ground each winter – do not remain in pots long enough to become root-bound; it is more likely to occur with shrubs and trees. If this appears to have happened, separate some of the soil from the root ball to encourage the roots to reach into the surrounding area. (Do not do this with conifers, however, as they must have as little root disturbance as possible.) Water each individual plant as soon as it is set in place, and water the entire garden when your planting is completed.

Now, mulch with an inch or more of ⅜-to-½-inch gravel, pebbles or stone chips chosen to blend with the rocks in the garden. Spread the mulch over the entire garden surface, making sure it is worked in under the mounds and clumps of plant leaves. This stone mulch is an important part of the garden. It keeps the soil cool and retains moisture, provides surface drainage, prevents mud from splashing on plants, discourages weeds and keeps the garden neat and trim. It protects plants that are vulnerable to moisture collection around their stems, and finally, it helps to unite the rocks with the plants. Many rock plants grow in this kind of gravelly mulch in the wild.

Planting a rock wall is different from planting a rock garden or raised bed. A rock wall provides all the features of the stone mulch while keeping vigorous plants under control. Many specimens look their best and last longest in this kind of structure. But each plant must have its roots firmly in contact with the soil behind the rocks or it will die. It is easiest to work with small plants, tucking them in carefully. Again, keep the larger, trailing plants away from the little gems, and be sure the soil around the roots receives enough water. Once established, plants in the rock wall will need little care.

In any rock garden that includes more than one or two species, labelling is wise. Unobtrusive labelling is important, as the markers can detract from the beauty of the garden. I have tried many methods and still do not have the perfect answer. One scheme is to make a plan on paper,

Labelling is wise but optional when only one or two distinct species are planted.

marking the location of each plant. Still, a small label should accompany each specimen. Push it down so that it does not show but can be pulled up if necessary. Or, in a small garden or planter box, use aluminum roofing nails painted white. With black waterproof, sunproof ink, mark each nail head with a number that corresponds to a list of names and numbers kept on paper. Plants tend to grow out and cover the nail heads, so be prepared to move the nails several times each year. Another method used by a 27 clever rock gardener involves painting plant names on small rocks with oil-based paint and setting the labelled rocks beside the appropriate plants. The stones can even be turned over so that the labels are entirely camouflaged.

Maintenance

Once the garden is planted, mulched and labelled, the job of keeping it all thriving begins. Ongoing jobs include:

•Watering. Carefully watch and water the garden for the first year after it has been planted, until the plants become well established. Thereafter, water thoroughly and deeply only when necessary.

•Weeding. Almost from the moment the garden is planted, weeding begins. It must be done by hand, as chemical herbicides cannot be used in the rock garden. The gravel mulch will help hold weeds down and make it easier to pull them up, but it is amazing how a weed can remain hidden or become a compact rosette mimicking the foliage of a prized plant. Try to avoid standing on the soil, and instead, step on a few well-placed rocks. Weeding a garden is not necessarily all work; close inspection of each plant gives you a chance to appreciate it again.

•Pruning. In early spring, remove all dead foliage. Then, as soon as the spreading plants such as phlox, aurinia and iberis have finished blooming, cut them back severely, or else they will last only a few years. Other plants will need to be thinned out or trimmed back in order to stay neat and compact. In most cases, you will want to remove seed heads after flowering. However, let the heads mature if you intend to save seeds or if they are attractive, as is the case with *Dryas octopetala* and *Anemone pulsatilla*, for instance.

•Winter Cover. Once the ground has frozen, protect plants, especially those of questionable hardiness or those subject to winter damage, by covering them with salt hay, evergreen branches or any light and airy material. This is particularly important in areas where the snow does not last all winter, as the soil may alternately freeze and thaw, which is bad for the plants. Try to apply this mulch so that the garden still has a neat appearance. Each year, after the ground has frozen, I cover the garden with the branches from our Christmas tree. The evergreen limbs look good all winter and are easy to remove in the spring.

•Spring Cleaning. If winter cover has been used, remove it a little at a time so that sun and air are let in gradually. Dead and straggly foliage should be removed and dead plants taken out. Shake the soil off their roots. This is a good time to replace plants or to move those that have become too exposed or too shaded. Remember to change labels accordingly. If any plants have been heaved out by frosts, carefully push them back into the ground. Weed if necessary. Add a little top dressing (a mixture of coarse sand or gravel, leaf mould and loam) around each plant, gently working it into the rosettes and mats as well. Add more gravel mulch as needed. Ericaceous plants (rhododendrons, azaleas, heathers and their relatives) should have an acidic top dressing of composted fallen leaves, known as leaf mould.

•Fertilizing. Most rock garden plants do not need to be fertilized. The top dressing described above is sufficient. Primroses and gentians, however, appreciate a little compost or well-rotted manure. After a few years, plants may begin to look poor, but often dividing or just pruning back will revive them. If you do apply fertilizer, do so in moderation and in spring. Otherwise, plants may not survive winter.

•Replacing Plants. Each year, there may be bare spaces where plants have died. Even though most rock garden plants are perennials – plants that live more than two years – that does not mean they will live forever. Many are naturally short-lived, some will not prove as hardy as hoped,

Ericaceous plants such as heathers should be top-dressed with composted leaves.

their own plants or from wild plants (see Resources). Often, seeds will be the only way to obtain rare plants. And sometimes, a seedling of a difficult plant will survive in the garden although a mature plant obtained from a nursery would not.

Problem Solving

Invasive plants, which can overrun a rock garden, should be avoided, especially in small areas. Some of these plants have spreading top growth that covers the surface and smothers smaller plants. Others spread by underground suckers or may send down roots wherever a piece of leaf or stem falls. Some, such as certain violets, produce hundreds of seedlings, which are annoying to pull out. Likewise, a plant recommended as a good ground cover is usually a poor choice for the rock garden. *Sedum sarmentosum* (stringy stonecrop) and *Sedum acre* (goldmoss sedum) are two such plants. Others to avoid are *Campanula rapunculoides* (a rapidly extending bellflower), *Aegopodium podagraria* (goutweed) and ferns with spreading roots such as hay-scented, lady and sensitive ferns and bracken. Even reliable, familiar plants such as candytuft, moss pinks and others mentioned earlier may become too large for the small garden. Instead, use the smaller species of these plants such as *Iberis sempervirens* 'Pygmaea' (dwarf candytuft) and *Phlox subulata* 'Sneewichen' (a miniature white phlox). The following chapter lists appropriate plants for the rock garden.

others will eventually become leggy in spite of yearly pruning, and still others may grow out of scale with the rest of the plants and require removal. Some specimens simply may not live up to the descriptions in the books you read.

The easiest way to keep a supply of replacement plants on hand is to propagate them yourself. Propagation is, I think, the most interesting part of gardening, especially of this sort. The subject is covered in many rock gardening books; there is not room for me to go into it here. But try to find space for a small nursery area for seedlings and a sand frame for cuttings. Once you have a few plants, you will have all you need to increase them either by division, taking cuttings or growing new plants from seed.

•Obtaining Seeds. The American Rock Garden Society and similar organizations have exchanges that allow one to obtain seeds collected by members either from

Aggressive plants are not the only things that are apt to overrun the garden. Voles and pine mice have caused problems in several places. I have tried poisoned bait and traps and filling their holes with gravel; nothing seems to work all of the time. Some years, there will be many holes and much damage to plants, usually my favourites. Other years, there are few signs of the intruders. So far, they have never appeared in raised beds. Garden 29

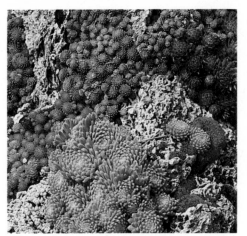

The waxy leaves of succulent plants such as sempervivums retain a water supply.

pests also include such insects as wood lice (sow bugs), which congregate under damp foliage and can become a nuisance, damaging the roots. Other insects that appear occasionally are aphids, lacewings, leaf miners and spider mites. Spray only when necessary and only those plants affected, but stop these insects before they spread to the rest of the garden.

Slugs, possibly the worst pests in the rock garden, can destroy a plant overnight and are particularly fond of species of the genus *Campanula* – the rarer the better, it seems. Either go out at night and pick them off the plants, spread slug bait around the vulnerable plants, or try leaving a small amount of beer in a low container nearby – the slugs are attracted to this and usually drown in the beer overnight.

Difficult Alpines

I have left for the last a word about the plants that, sooner or later, every gardener wants to try – the true alpines, which grow above the timberline on mountains or in the polar zones, some of the most beautiful and sought-after of all plants. And, of course, also the most difficult to grow.

In their native habitat, these plants have adapted to winter cold and summer drought by growing in attractive low mats, cushions or tufts and by forming long taproots to reach for water deep in their native rocky scree. They have large, brilliant flowers to attract insects, and their leaves are often equipped to survive the harsh conditions on the mountain. Hairiness, for instance, helps leaves avoid desiccation, while succulence allows leaves to retain their own water supply within a waxy, water-resistant outer covering. These adaptations, paradoxically, can also make the plants difficult to grow. Sitting in water will kill most alpines, which are adapted only to dealing with drought. Little or no snow cover in winter can be devastating. Even if the plants survive winter, they often fail in what rock gardener Lincoln Foster calls the "muggs" of summer. Last year, my husband and I built two planters at our summer home in Maryland. They were planted this spring and kept watered during a very dry summer. Most plants survived, but I lost several tiny alpines, probably due to the heat.

Some alpines, in fact, will never be able to survive away from their homes. These are the ones to visit and enjoy in the mountains. *Eritrichium nanum*, which famous rock gardener Reginald Farrer called "king of the mountains," comes from the high peaks of Europe and America and is a plant with tiny, fuzzy, thick leaves and small, beautiful, deep blue forget-me-not flowers. It is rare to hear of anyone growing it for more than a few years. Other alpines are difficult but often can be made to survive, provided sufficient care is taken to reproduce their native habitat. An approximation of the high alpine scree or the glacial moraine can be created, for instance, as described in the previous chapter. The general idea is to have a mixture of gravel, loam and peat that will provide a deep root run and keep the tops of the plants dry. A sand bed is another way to grow the plants. It is a

While some alpines cannot survive beyond their native slopes, there are others, just as lovely, *that can be coaxed along, such as* Gentiana verna.

mixture of fine pebbles, grit and small amounts of sand and humus or just sharp sand spread about 8 inches thick over regular garden soil. This is similar to, but finer than, a scree mix but provides like conditions for the plants and can be used to establish new or difficult plants.

Some enthusiasts grow their plants in a special kind of greenhouse known as an alpine house, which provides more ventilation than a regular greenhouse and has winter temperatures usually kept just above freezing. Plants that are not resistant to frost or cannot tolerate damp winter conditions grow well here. Plants such as Kabschia saxifrages, which bloom in late winter, are safer to raise and easier to enjoy in an alpine house. And desert plants and certain bulbs, which need to be dry in summer, can be kept here. The plants are usually confined to individual pots, but an entire rock garden could be built on a bench. My husband and I once maintained such a miniature garden on the centre bench of a conventional greenhouse kept at about 40 degrees F all winter. A pump circulated water around a streambed built of fibreglass and sand, the surface was mulched with moss, and tiny rhododendrons and cassiopes bloomed each year. Eventually, the plants became too large and were planted outdoors, but this garden gave us pleasure for more than five years.

Whether I live in the country or the city and whether I am cultivating a greenhouse bed, a chink in a wall or a small planter box, the rock garden with its lovely quiet plants has become an irreplaceable part of my life.

Marnie Flook is an archivist for and former director of the American Rock Garden Society. She also approaches rock gardening as a writer, lecturer, educator and photographer.

Chapter Four:
Rock Garden Plants from A to Z

"It is a new language to a clever linguist, wherein, when he has learned it from A to Z (from anemone to zephyranthes), he finds poetry sublime and sweet. Oh! those . . . harbingers of spring, those anemones . . . those sheets of aubrieta, arabis, iberis . . . those sedums, saxifrages, sempervivums and other jewels, countless as the harlequin comfits upon a Christmas cake . . . ." ∞ The lavish phraseology of Dean Hole in describing the spring rock garden seems quaint, or perhaps ridiculous, to our tastes. And yet, the beguiling miniatures of the rock garden do invite description, and here it is easy enough for a certain lyricism to invade even our unsentimental age. There are many factors accounting for the close-knit ranks of alpine lovers and the camaraderie engendered in rock garden societies, but surely the characteristics of the plants themselves are at the heart of the matter. ∞ Five rock garden specialists from across the continent were asked to submit their comments on a list of rock garden plants, most (though not all) suitable for a newcomer to the genre. Since growing conditions in different parts of the continent vary greatly, the climatic zone maps of Canada and the United States, which appear on pages 85 and 86, will enable you to identify your own zone and hence discover how the plants may be expected to behave for you. Some basic information on 33 cultivation, care and propagation is provided. A final section of supplementary notes forms an introduction to ferns, grasses, annuals, dwarf shrubs and conifers to round out the microcosm of the rock garden.

The contributors, listed geographically from east to west, will be identified by their initials in the pages following.

B.J. Bernard S. Jackson, curator, The Memorial University Botanical Garden at Oxen Pond, St. John's, Newfoundland. Agriculture Canada climatic zone 5b; United States Department of Agriculture (USDA) zone 5.

T.C. Trevor Cole, curator, Dominion Arboretum, Plant Research Centre, Ottawa, Ontario. Agriculture Canada climatic zone 5a; USDA zone 4.

A.P. Allen Paterson, director, Royal Botanical Gardens, Hamilton, Ontario. Agriculture Canada climatic zone 6b; USDA zone 6.

P.K. Panayoti Kelaidis, curator, Rock Alpine Garden, Denver Botanic Gardens, Denver, Colorado; and Gwen Kelaidis, landscape designer, specialist in trough gardens and native American alpines. USDA zone 5; Agriculture Canada climatic zone 5b.

G.S. Gerald Straley, research scientist and curator of collections, The University of British Columbia Botanical Garden, University of British Columbia, Vancouver, British Columbia. Agriculture Canada climatic zone 9a; USDA zone 8.

The plants are listed alphabetically in two groupings: Herbaceous Perennials; and Bulbs (including Corms, Rhizomes and Tubers). An asterisk(*) marks those that are illustrated.

Herbaceous Perennials

Achillea ageratifolia; A. tomentosa

(yarrow)

Achilles, hero of ancient Greek mythology, is said to have made use of these plants medicinally – hence their name. Greenish grey aromatic leaves are characteristic of this large genus of the north temperate zone, which includes a number of dwarf species that form mats or tufts and are very much at home in the rock garden. Among them, *Achillea ageratifolia*, growing wild on the slopes of southern Europe, has feathery leaves and large clear white flowers; more familiar is *A. tomentosa,** woolly yarrow, with its tufts of downy foliage and flat plates of butter-yellow on 6-inch stalks. Good in dry walls and scree. Give them a lean, well-drained soil in full sun; propagate by division of older clumps or by cuttings in spring or summer.

B.J. The genus appears to hate our wet snow and is somewhat temperamental here. Nonetheless, *Achillea ageratifolia* and another dwarf yarrow, *A. argentea*, are both showing great promise in our rock garden. They are delightful plants with many long-lasting, daisylike flowers.

T.C. Very good carpeting plants that would still be worth growing even if they didn't have attractive spring flowers. The finely cut foliage gives an almost ferny appearance. If flowers are cut off and not allowed to set seed, the plants will often rebloom.

A.P. Good tufts of silvery foliage.

P.K. *Achillea ageratifolia* is ideally suited to the Rocky Mountain region since it needs less supplemental moisture than most rock plants and is attractive year-round. Sometimes considered a subspecies of the former, *A. sibirica* has larger marguerites and whiter foliage. *Achillea tomentosa* is widely available, with vivid yellow flowers, but is deciduous.

G.S. The very low-growing mounds of silvery leaves are attractive even when the flower clusters are not open. Not very commonly grown in the Vancouver area, except in botanical gardens and by alpine enthusiasts.

Aethionema spp

(stone-cress, Persian candytuft)

The stone-cresses, members of the mustard family and mostly natives of the Mediterranean region, have small, narrow blue-grey leaves and spring-blooming flowers ranging through various shades of pink. Undoubtedly the loveliest, with its rich rose colour and compact habit, is *Aethionema warleyense** (*A.* 'Warley Rose'). The stone-cresses do well in sunny rock crevices, dry walls and scree, in comparatively dry, sandy-loamy soil. They may be propagated by seed or by cuttings taken in summer.

B.J. The only species I have seen growing in my area is *Aethionema coridifolium*. It is somewhat tender and suffers from winter dieback, but if the dead material is cut off in spring, the plant seems to bounce back well enough. A really beautiful little plant well worth some effort to have blooming in the garden.

T.C. These are really subshrubs with woody stems and persistent leaves. I have not had very great success with them in Ottawa, but just a few miles away, they thrive and seed themselves. The showiest is 'Warley Rose'; easier to obtain is seed of the two species *Aethionema armenum* and *A. grandiflorum*, from Asia Minor and Persia, respectively. The former is only 4 inches tall and is the parent of 'Warley Rose.' *Aethionema grandiflorum* grows about 1 foot tall and has rose flowers in July. In areas where the winter temperature does not go below minus 20 degrees F, stone-cresses can be a valuable addition for summer colour.

A.P. 'Warley Rose' is probably the best – brilliant rose pink heads, grey-blue foliage.

P.K. The most widely cultivated species are *Aethionema pulchellum* and *A. grandiflorum*. They form condensed subshrubs with metallic silvery leaves that are covered for weeks in late spring with a blanket of luminous pink crosses. These form flattened seed heads that are interesting in their own right, as they split apart scattering seed far and wide – self-sown seedlings are rarely a nuisance in the garden. *Aethionema* tolerates a wide range of conditions but prefers sun.

G.S. Not as well known as it should be.

Alchemilla alpina

(Lady's mantle)

A member of the rose family, alchemilla grows throughout temperate Europe, Asia and parts of North America. It is thought that the genus takes its name from the mediaeval science of alchemy, 35

wherein magical properties were ascribed to the droplets of moisture beading the leaves. The common name, too, may have a mediaeval origin, in the belief that the draperies of the Virgin Mary are echoed in the pleated silvery leaves themselves. Indeed, the plant is grown more for its attractive leaves than for its rather inconspicuous flowers. It forms a dense mat or carpet and grows easily in any ordinary garden soil. Propagate by division.

B.J. I have not seen this plant growing in Newfoundland, but since *Alchemilla vulgaris* and *A. mollis** grow extremely well here, I feel that this compact little species would be well worth a trial.

T.C. Not a very spectacular rock garden plant, but useful for shaded areas. It grows about 6 inches high and has greenish flowers. Tends to self-sow and can become invasive, crowding out more desirable plants.

A.P. Elegant pleated leaves hold aloft pearl-like raindrops under sprays of greenish flowers.

P.K. Does particularly well in rich soils and partial shade. The flowers are negligible – small chartreuse stars; it is the foliage that is of paramount interest. Will not tolerate drought.

G.S. The rounded, lobed leaves of soft green with silver undersides are attractive throughout the summer and complement other textures of foliage in the alpine garden. Spikes of small green flowers are not showy but interesting.

Alyssum alpestre; A. saxatile

(basket-of-gold, madwort)

Ranging from the Mediterranean to Siberia, these plants of the mustard family, with their profuse bloom and often prostrate growth, are basic to the rock garden. They are often at their best in dry walls and fissures, where they are less likely to become invasive. The dwarf *Alyssum alpestre*, from the European Alps, forms a mound of closely grouped silvery leaves with copious pale yellow flowers. *Alyssum saxatile** (now more generally listed as *Aurinia saxatilis*), a native of central and southern Europe, has brilliant yellow flowers and is more sprawling. Both plants prefer a sunny site and well-drained soil, not overly rich. Propagate by seed or by cuttings in June.

B.J. Our trials with *Alyssum alpestre* are currently inconclusive. *Alyssum saxatile* has been popular in my area for generations; the cultivar 'Compactum' is excellent. The plant benefits from a moderate shearing as soon as the flowers have died. *Alyssum montanum* and *A. wulfenianum* are far superior for the small rock garden. They require very well-drained soil in full sun. Be careful not to overfeed them, and shear off the dead flower heads immediately. Great plants for the scree.

T.C. A very brash, garish group of plants that, while they give a bright show for a few days, make you pay for the pleasure by seeding themselves with reckless abandon. Just about the only way to grow these plants is to shear the tops off as soon as the flowers fade. They are best displayed trailing over a low stone wall. There are several named forms that are only just hardy to minus 20 degrees F and are killed off in Ottawa every five or six years. Seed-exchange lists reveal a multitude of *Alyssum* species, but none that I have tried have been more than "interesting"; many are weedy.

A.P. *Alyssum saxatile* is an excellent type for dry walls but too robust for most rock gardens; a better, softer-hued cultivar is 'Citrinum.' Clip it after flowering to encourage decent shape and summer foliage.

P.K. We haven't grown *Alyssum alpestre*, but the similar *A. montanum* and *A. wulfenianum* are widely grown in Rocky Mountain gardens. They have much neater mats than the better-known *Aurinia saxatilis* and are just as colourful in full bloom. They tolerate very hot and dry conditions and add to the noisy yellow tone of spring in the rock garden.

G.S. These and other species of *Alyssum* (some split off into a separate genus, *Aurinia*) are widely available here and very easy to grow in the rock garden or in rock walls. *Aurinia saxatilis*, along with the related species of *Iberis*, *Arabis* and *Aubrieta*, is the most common rockery plant in our area. They are care-free, available and therefore overused. Bright yellow flowers and evergreen ("evergrey") foliage are attractive.

Androsace sarmentosa

(rock jasmine)

Members of the primrose family, androsaces are mainly mountain plants from Europe, Asia and temperate North America; *Androsace sarmentosa** ranges from the Himalayas to western China. From a central rosette of silvery foliage, elegant, primulalike rose-coloured flower heads emerge in early summer, and runners stretch out to establish new growth. It does best in a sunny moraine, where it is likely to remain compact, but will also grow in normal rock garden soil and can take some shade; good drainage is important. Propagation is by division of the rosettes or by seed.

B.J. This beautiful, easily propagated little plant is the only androsace that we have found to be hardy in our area. The variety we have is *watkinsii*. It can be a little temperamental in our fickle climate, so it is a wise plan to have a couple of back-up plants overwinter in the cold frame. Indications are that it does best for us in light shade in a sand, peat and leaf mould growing medium. Though its heavy scent is reminiscent of tomcats, its flowers can be borne in great profusion and at such times put on an excellent show.

T.C. This plant only seems happy when it is growing in a rock crevice. Planted in an open pocket, it gradually shrivels and dies, but when tucked into a crack between two rocks, the plant thrives and spreads out along the join lines. There are several closely related species that differ mainly in their difficulty of cultivation; none are plants for the novice.

P.K. Extremely tolerant of a wide range of conditions, as long as it has sufficient moisture. The pink clusters last for a long time. *Androsace sempervivoides* is just as easy to grow, with symmetrical green rosettes. There are also many other aristocratic androsaces that do well in Colorado in cool crevices with occasional irrigation.

G.S. This and several other species in the genus are grown for their spreading habit, forming low mounds of silvery-leaved rosettes and showy flowers ranging from white to dark pink. Fairly easy to grow and not seen as often as they should be.

Aquilegia spp

(columbine)

Columbines, members of the buttercup family, are natives of the north temperate zone. Many of the smaller species such as *Aquilegia alpina* (from the European Alps) and *A. flabellata* (from Japan) are suitable for the rock garden, where their delicate lobed leaves and colourful spurred blooms are shown to advantage. A rocky soil with sun or some shade suits them well, and they need ample moisture from spring through early summer. Since they tend to interbreed, propagation by division of clumps in spring is sometimes more reliable than by seed.

B.J. Where would a rock garden be without its columbines? *Aquilegia alpina, A. einseleana, A. bertolonii,* * *A. saximontana* and *A. scopulorum* have grown well for us. *Aquilegia flabellata nana-alba* makes lovely domes of blue-green foliage, but I find its white flowers disappointing. However, *A. flabellata pumila* (syn. *A. akitensis*) should be in every rock garden. If I had to pick one aquilegia for a small rock garden, this would be it.

T.C. A large number of columbines are suitable for the rock garden, and an even larger number are not. Aquilegias have no morals, and any plants that are raised from seed should be treated with suspicion until their eventual size is known. One of the best and most reliable from seed is the dwarf fan columbine *Aquilegia flabellata nana* and its white form *nana-alba*. This usually seems to come true from seed and grows only 6 inches tall, with flowers that are up to 1 inch across. The alpine columbine (*A. alpina*) is the same height, but not all the seed lots I have tried have been true to type. Growing only 3 inches tall, *A. saximontana* from the Rockies thrives in well-drained scree and blooms for much of the summer, but it is not a plant for the novice.

A.P. *Aquilegia alpina* 'Hensol Harebell' is a particularly good form.

P.K. Practically all columbines do well in partial shade or in a sunny scree in Rocky Mountain gardens, although we naturally have a preference for our native species such as the adaptable and fragrant *Aquilegia caerulea* and the tiny huddled *A. saximontana*, which blooms over a long season in the garden. Our favourite exotics are *A. bertolonii*, in its small forms, and the waxy-leaved Japanese *A. flabellata*.

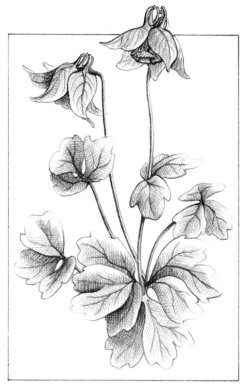

G.S. The shorter, blue-flowered species, including *Aquilegia alpina*, *A. pyrenaica* and *A. flabellata*, are suitable for the rock garden and quite nice when in flower in spring. *Aquilegia flabellata* has naturalized very freely in the alpine garden at the UBC Botanical Garden.

Arabis alpina; A. caucasica

(rock cress)

These members of the mustard family are widely spread over the northern hemisphere – the genus name alludes to Arabia, where some species are native. The most common rock cress, *Arabis caucasica*, produces loose mats of greenish grey foliage and ample clusters of small white, pink or purplish flowers; *A. alpina** is a more compact version with white flowers. Both are good in dry walls and ledges. They flower in spring and require plenty of sun and well-drained soil. Propagate by division of the roots in spring or fall.

B.J. *Arabis alpina* is an ideal plant for the beginner. We use the white variety 'Grandiflora' and the pink *A. a. rosea*. *Arabis albida* does well in our area, but *A. blepharophylla*, *A. lucida* and *A. variegata* have all shown a definite dislike either of our winters or of me. Give rock cress a good haircut as soon as the flowers are finished, to keep them compact and floriferous.

T.C. Favourite spring-flowering plants for the small rock garden, they should be lightly sheared after flowering to promote new growth for the following year. There are both double-flowered and variegated forms of the Caucasian rock cress, as well as pink-flowered varieties of each.

A.P. The inevitable associates of *Alyssum saxatile* and just as easy. Again, apt to be too robust for the specialist garden. The double forms are longer- 39 lasting in flower and must be propagated vegetatively.

P.K. *Arabis caucasica* makes a fine ground cover for sunny or shady corners with impoverished soils and unpredictable precipitation; for the rock garden proper, we prefer the more congested *A. carduchorum* or the tiny, woolly-leaved *A. bryoides*.

G.S. The more usual species cultivated in Vancouver rock gardens and cascading out of wall crevices is *A. caucasica* and its various named forms; it is very easy to grow and is pest-free. A number of other *Arabis* species are available from specialists or seed exchanges and are seen in the Vancouver area from time to time. There are also many native species here, but most of these are not especially garden-worthy.

Arenaria spp

(sandwort)

The sandworts, members of the pink family found only in the north temperate zone, are small mosslike plants with tiny flowers that grow in neat tufts; they are well suited to the wall or paving-stone garden and need open sunshine and sandy or gritty soil. (The name "arenaria" means "growing in sandy places.") They are summer-flowering and easily propagated by root division.

B.J. If you like sparkling, pure white flowers, *Arenaria montana* is difficult to beat. It is easily and quickly grown from seed, but as we lose a percentage of our plants each winter, a few backup plants are indicated. With its soft purple flowers, *A. purpurascens* is an excellent choice but may be difficult to acquire. *Arenaria verna** and *A. v. caespitosa*, now more usually classed under the genus *Minuartia*, are easily grown and are useful between paving slabs and in the nooks and crannies of stone steps.

T.C. These are easily taken for mosses until the tiny, white starlike flowers ap-

pear. One of the most showy is *Arenaria verna aurea*, which is bright yellow when grown in full sun. Many of the species are weedy and tend to be invasive, while others, such as *A. fendleri*, are delightful compact plants in their native Rockies, although they grow much taller at lower elevations.

A.P. *Arenaria balearica* is one of the loveliest of all rock garden plants. It will spread over most walls and rocks. *Arenaria verna* makes a tidy cushion of tiny leaves; *A. v. aurea* is a useful gold form. Both need open positions to retain shape.

P.K. *Arenaria tetraquetra*, a congested cushion, is surprisingly adaptable in our climate to any good gritty soil in sun or partial shade and forms a superb specimen in a few years. *Arenaria montana*, with its large mound of deep green leaves and white stars in early summer, is widely available from local nurseries. It prefers loamy soils.

G.S. Several of these mosslike or grasslike plants, with their wiry stems and small white flowers, are grown here. Most are not very showy but are relatively easy to grow in well-drained soils.

Armeria maritima; A. juniperifolia

(thrift)

Armerias belong to the plumbago family and, in their wild state, grow throughout most of the northern hemisphere and parts of South America. They are mat-forming, tufted evergreen plants with their leaves in dense rosettes – the stiff flower stalks support globe-shaped flower heads. *Armeria maritima*,* found naturally in Europe, Asia and North America, has flower stalks about 4 inches tall; *A. juniperifolia*, a native of Spain, is a more compact species with rather prickly foliage and flower stalks 1 to 2 inches high. They prefer a light sandy soil and are easily propagated by division.

B.J. Both these plants are useful in the St. John's area. The dark red and white varieties of *Armeria maritima* are particularly desirable. They require full sun and deep, well-drained soil. Large old clumps have a tendency to die out in the centre. *Armeria juniperifolia* (syn. *A. caespitosa*) makes hard, compact hummocks and is a must for the serious rock gardener. It does best for me when planted in a scree but is also ideal for a trough. Indications are that it should be protected from the west and southwest winds of our spring. 'Bevans Variety' is especially pleasing. Plant armerias when they are small, and do not move them.

T.C. The main drawback with this plant is that it grows. Planted as a neat little hummock, it spreads outward and ends up as a mat a foot or more across, which then starts to die out in the centre, giving it an untidy look. Luckily, it is easy to propagate, and pieces pulled off the outside root quickly.

A.P. The smaller forms with tight hummocks are admirable. Spherical heads of pale to vivid pink in early summer; 'Bees Pink' a good form.

P.K. *Armeria maritima* blooms over a long season in the garden, particularly if kept trimmed of old bloom. The tiniest forms approach the spiny-leaved Spanish *A. juniperifolia*, which is a scree-loving plant for cool, sunny gardens.

G.S. Very easy and very common in our area. A standard for all rock gardens. Dense tufts of grasslike leaves form round mounds or, eventually, undulating carpets of dark green, making a good foil for the bright pink flowers.

Aster alpinus

(rock aster)

The true aster is only distantly related to the annual garden, or China, aster. It belongs to an enormous genus, of which a number of the smaller species are suited to the rock garden. *Aster alpinus*,* from the mountains of Europe and the Rockies, is 6 inches to 1 foot tall, the solitary flower heads appearing in late spring from rosettes of spatula-shaped leaves. Give it a well-drained, not-too-rich soil, and divide after flowering.

B.J. They can be a bit temperamental in my area but should be given a try, for 41 if you find the right soil for them, they are lovely. They like full sun and somewhat moist but well-drained soil. The variety 'Rosea' sprouts nice pink buds, and 'Albus' produces white flowers; the varieties with deep violet blooms and golden centres are possibly the most effective.

T.C. This is the most dependable of the small asters that are suitable for the rock garden. It seems to live longer if dug up and divided every three or four years. Closely related are several Asiatic species, such as *Aster farreri* and *A. himalaicus*, which have survived several winters in Ottawa. *Aster alpinus* flowers for a number of weeks before most of the native asters, so seed generally comes true to type.

A.P. *Aster alpinus* brings easy, reliable daisies in early summer.

P.K. Comparatively large violet daisies over a neat rosette of deep green leaves. A valuable and adaptable plant for either loamy or scree soils.

G.S. One of the easiest and smallest of

a very large genus, most species of which are better suited to the perennial garden. In late spring, *Aster alpinus* produces single flower heads on short stems, each bloom with purple to white rays surrounding a yellow centre.

Aubrieta deltoidea

(purple rock cress)

Another member of the mustard family, *Aubrieta* is closely related to *Arabis* and *Alyssum*, and together they form a sort of triumvirate of the rock garden. It is a native of the Mediterranean and Asia Minor, with crowded, mat-forming leaves and blossoms of purple or violet. Happy in a wall or crevice, it needs a stony soil. Cut back after flowering; propagate by seed, cuttings or spring or fall division.

B.J. *Aubrieta deltoidea** is extremely unreliable in my area. Some gardens can grow it, others cannot, and I don't know why. There are so many other beautiful plants that respond to my efforts and grow well for me that I've given up, for the time being, on this particular species.

T.C. One of the most popular of rock plants, even with people who don't have a rock garden. Cutting back severely as soon as flowering is finished will keep the plant within bounds and stop it from growing so large that it smothers nearby plants. Easy to grow from seed.

A.P. The third of the *Alyssum/Arabis* axis. Wonderful range of colours; singles and doubles for spring display where there is plenty of room.

P.K. A standby for spring colour. Does very well in partial shade in our climate but needs a little extra moisture in full sun. Long-lived.

G.S. Another basic plant, which is readily available in several different forms (from pale to dark pink and purple, with green or variegated foliage) and is care-free and very easy to grow.

Campanula spp

(bellflower)

The large genus *Campanula*, widely distributed in the northern hemisphere, includes a number of dwarf species with creeping or mounding tendencies, making them ideal for the rock garden. Many are long-flowering, and their bell-like blossoms (predominantly blue, though occasionally white) can be a particular pleasure when the riot of their spring-blooming neighbours has died down. They flourish in walls, paving cracks and ledges, with some shade and cool, damp (but not wet), gritty earth. Propagate by seed.

B.J. It is hard to imagine a rock garden without a variety of bellflowers. *Campanula carpatica, C. cochlearifolia,* * *C. glomerata acaulis, C. barbata* and *C. finitima* do well for me. The native *C. rotundifolia* comes easily from wild collected seed and is very beautiful; we also have an interesting double-flowered bellflower bought as *C. warleyensis*, which is charming but hard to find. *Campanula garganica* 'Hirsuta' has lovely blue stars instead of bells but falls easy prey to slugs. *Campanula sartori* is one of my favourites but unfortunately is a monocarp (a plant that bears fruit once and dies), so let it self-seed. It needs to be grown in a wall, so blow the seeds into the cracks.

T.C. *Campanula carpatica* is the best

known of the many bellflowers suitable for the rock garden. It forms neat mounds and is especially useful since it flowers later in the summer when the main floral display is finished. There are several named forms in a range of blue and white shades. Over the years, it has proved very long-lived in Ottawa. Three other bell-flowers should also be considered. *Campanula portenschlagiana* (Dalmatian bell-flower) and *C. poscharskyana* are trailing species that are good for cascading over rock faces. The first has purplish flowers and the second, pale blue. In very well-drained areas, the miniature *C. cochlearifolia* will thrive. This species grows only 2 to 3 inches tall and spreads slowly if given the right conditions. There is a large number of other bellflowers suitable for the rock garden; most of these are easy to raise from seed.

A.P. The low, spreading *Campanula portenschlagiana* and trailing *C. poscharskyana* are valuable for rock garden use; forms of *C. carpatica* are small enough for inclusion.

P.K. Important for summer colour, almost all campanulas are easily grown here. *Campanula portenschlagiana* does 43 best in a gritty soil with some shade, while *C. garganica*, with similar foliage, does well in full sun. The monocarpic Lycrata group of this genus offers gorgeous rosettes and has also proved quite successful here.

G.S. Some of our best alpine garden plants are found in this genus. There are dozens of species and varieties grown here; many are common and very easy, while others are collectors' items and more difficult to grow.

Cerastium tomentosum; C. alpinum

(snow-in-summer)

Cerastium tomentosum, an attractive but invasive species, has its place in rock gardening as a warning against the use of overly aggressive plants in the rock garden. Its grey foliage, profuse white flowers and fiercely spreading habit make it an excellent choice as a ground cover; but in the rock garden, it should yield to its more restrained relative, *C. alpinum,** a compact native of arctic, subarctic and alpine parts of Europe, which may be raised from seed or increased by division. It prefers a porous, humus-rich soil.

B.J. *Cerastium tomentosum?* I would not allow this aggressive little bandit anywhere near my rock garden. Everybody and their granny will try to give you this plant, but harden your heart and say *NO!!*

T.C. One of the most widely grown alpines, *Cerastium tomentosum*, or snow-in-summer, is also probably one of the most widely cursed. It is invasive and will seed itself into the middle of other plants and slowly choke them out. Treat it with care. Much more desirable is *C. alpinum lanatum*, with woolly foliage and short spikes of white flowers. While it doesn't give quite the floral display that snow-in-summer does, it is not nearly as invasive.

A.P. *Cerastium tomentosum* is best as a ground cover above spring bulbs in dryish banks.

P.K. Choice alpines should not be afflicted with the company of *Cerastium tomentosum*; its cousin *C. alpinum lanatum*, however, is an elegant and restrained cushion, fit for the best society.

G.S. Although extremely common and easily grown here, *Cerastium tomentosum* is, perhaps, too invasive for small gardens and needs periodic trimming to keep it within bounds.

Dianthus caesius; D. alpinus

(pink)

Many of the small pinks are welcome inhabitants of the rock garden, with their mats of grass-green or grey foliage and white to pink or rose-purple blossoms, often fragrant and fringed or crimson-eyed. Give them a well-drained gritty soil in full sun; propagate by seed or cuttings.

B.J. The true *Dianthus caesius* is probably unavailable, and all sorts of junk now turns up under this name, so beware. *Dianthus alpinus* is a real gem and does well for us if a certain type of beetle larva does not bore into its crown. Other dwarf pinks that like our area are *D. arvernensis*, *D. la bourbrille*, *D. neglectus* and *D. squarrosus*. *Dianthus haematocalyx* does best in a scree and when in flower has to be seen to be believed. Don't forget the maiden pink, *D. deltoides*,* especially if you are a beginner. Some people look down on it, but I personally could just not imagine a rock garden without this bright, good-natured little plant. It grows easily and quickly from seed, and the seed is easy to buy.

T.C. *Dianthus caesius, D. alpinus* and *D. deltoides* are the three most common of the many species of *Dianthus* suitable for the rock garden. All are very easy to raise from seed, but the resulting plants may vary in flower colour and shape. Several seedlings should be grown so that good colour forms can be selected.

A.P. Full sun and good drainage are essential for all pinks. Add *Dianthus deltoides* to the list. All are good in cracks between paving.

P.K. Tolerant of heat and drought and easily grown from seed and cuttings, the pinks are a mainstay of the early summer garden here. *Dianthus caesius* (syn. *D. gratianopolitanus*) 'Tiny Rubies' is long-lived. The largest flowering miniature pinks are *D. alpinus* and *D. callizonus*, which like a gritty soil in sun. The best tight cushions are *D. erinaceus, D. simu-*

lans, D. subacaulis and *D. freynii*, grown primarily for their form.

G.S. Another large genus with many easy species; a must for any rock garden.

Dicentra eximia

(wild bleeding heart)

Wild bleeding hearts belong to a small genus that is mostly North American and mostly suited to the deep shade and moist conditions of a wild woodland garden. However, *Dicentra eximia** will settle in the rock garden, given semi-shade and moisture-retaining soil, and its feathery leaves and nodding blossoms are delicately attractive additions. Propagate by division in early spring – or after foliage has died – or by seed. It does not enjoy being transplanted.

B.J. I believe this plant to be more suited for growing at the front of a perennial border or other such place, rather than in a rock garden.

T.C. A dwarf form of the more common Dutchman's breeches that likes a semi-shaded site. The closely related western bleeding heart (*Dicentra formosa*) spreads slowly by underground runners. 45

Both have survived well in Ottawa, but they are probably not suitable for many rock gardens.

A.P. The smallest of the bleeding hearts; give them peaty soil and at least half shade. A grey-leaved form has been named 'Spring Morning.'

P.K. Blooms on and off all summer in a moist, shady woodland.

G.S. This plant and forms of our native *Dicentra formosa* are good, easy perennials that like a cool or slightly shady place; without this, the foliage will sunburn in summer. Known better in Europe than in North America. The grey-green fernlike foliage is an attractive background for the pink to white flowers.

Dodecatheon alpinum

(shooting star)

Most of the 15 or so species of this lovely plant, a member of the primrose family, are native to western North America. *Dodecatheon alpinum*,* an inhabitant of moist mountain areas, bears cyclamen-like, nodding purple blossoms that die after flowering on 5-inch stalks arising from leaves in basal rosettes. It requires a moderately rich, non-limy, moist soil and light shade. Propagation may be by seed or by fall or spring division.

B.J. Not familiar with this plant in my area. *Dodecatheon meadia* does well in St. John's, but we grow it in rich organic soil in the light shade of our woodland bed.

T.C. North American plants found mainly in wet meadows and on snow-melt streamsides. In the rock garden, they need to be planted in association with other plants that will protect their root systems from summer heat once the foliage has died back. I planted them with *Aster alpinus*, which flowers later, and even on a dry site, they survived for several years.

A.P. All shooting stars are immediate attractions. This is the most available of the smaller species.

P.K. Here only *Dodecatheon pulchellum* is commonly grown. It does best in moist shade. Mark it well to prevent doing damage to it during its long dormancy.

G.S. This and several other species of charming little North American plants are often grown in rock gardens. Most prefer a slightly shady place. They need adequate moisture in winter and spring when they are growing, but most need to dry out in summer, a condition which our relatively drier summers provide naturally for them.

Draba aizoides

(whitlow grass)

A member of the mustard family, this native of northern and central European mountains and several of its sister species are among the earliest-blooming plants in the garden. Drabas need a gritty, somewhat limy soil with good drainage and are happy in dry walls and crevices. *Draba aizoides** produces bright yellow flowers 2 to 4 inches above a compact evergreen mound of bristly leaves.

B.J. This plant grows and flowers well in my area but is sometimes difficult to maintain as a nice-looking compact clump. The plant appears to like a sunny site and gritty, humusy soil that is not allowed to dry out. It is easily grown from seed, so it would not hurt to try a few of the many other species.

T.C. Every rock garden should have a hummock of bright yellow whitlow grass for early spring colour. There are many different species, and they can be divided roughly into tallish (white-flowered) and moundlike (yellow-flowered). They have been fairly short-lived in Ottawa, but there are usually a few self-sown seedlings growing close by to take over.

A.P. Tiny tussocks for growing in rock crevices. Not much show, but always fascinating.

P.K. Their vivid yellows – synonymous with the joy of early spring – begin their bright parade in late February or early March. *Draba aizoides, D. olympica* and *D. hispanica* are widely and easily grown

here. The tiny and more difficult choice cushions, such as *D. bryoides* and *D. mollissima*, require careful placement in gritty soil in crevices. *Draba rigida* is a superb, tight cushion that is usually the last to bloom in early summer.

G.S. This and several other drabas form very dense, rounded mounds with yellow or white flowers on slender stems. Does best in our area in a cool greenhouse or with some other protection from winter rains. Will grow outside in very well-drained soils in full sun.

Dryas octopetala

(mountain avens)

This small genus, with two of its estimated four species being solely natives of North America, is found widely throughout alpine and arctic regions of the northern hemisphere. The Latin "dryas" translates as "wood nymph," a suitably charming name for a plant that is not only very attractive but also fairly easy to grow. It is a subshrub of the rose family, a spreading, prostrate evergreen, with leaves dark green on top, downy white underneath; its solitary flower heads rise no more than 2 or 3 inches and become very decorative feathery plumes in the fruit stage. *Dryas octopetala,** found in North America but also in Europe and Asia, has white flowers with eight petals, as the name suggests. Dryases appreciate a coolish summer with full sun and well-drained, somewhat limy soil and may be propagated by seed or by summer cuttings.

B.J. This species does well for us but appears to grow better in a fairly organic soil. Maybe it requires that bit of extra moisture in summer. *Dryas octopetala* 'Minor' also grows well and would be more appropriate for the small rock garden. Our two native species, *D. drummondii* and *D. integrifolia*, are well worth growing if they become available to you. The latter is particularly suited to the small rock garden, as well as the alpine trough.

47

T.C. I have never had any great success with mountain avens. I have tried several different species, and while they have grown well for a time, eventually they have died. They thrive in the Arctic and at high elevations, so maybe they just don't like muggy summer weather.

A.P. Fine spreading subshrub – dark leaves and white flowers, like small up-facing roses.

P.K. A superb evergreen mat that blooms on and off all summer here. The larger forms can spread enough to become a menace in a small rock garden.

G.S. A mat-forming perennial with unusual, lobed, partially evergreen leaves and showy roselike white flowers followed by plumy seed heads. Likes a gravelly, very well-drained soil.

Gentiana acaulis; G. septemfida

(gentian)

Among the large genus *Gentiana*, the dwarf alpines of Europe are particularly outstanding rock garden plants. *Gentiana acaulis*,* the trumpet gentian, is one of these, its deep blue, single, upturned trumpet-blossoms arising from neat rosettes of glossy evergreen leaves in spring; it may, however, prove a capricious bloomer. *Gentiana septemfida*, found from Asia Minor to the Caucasus region of the U.S.S.R., has narrower bell-shaped flowers – clustered several to a stem and of a similar deep blue – which bloom later in the summer; it dies back during the winter. The latter is probably an easier and more reliable species for an introduction to a somewhat temperamental genus. Gentians require a humus-rich, well-drained but sufficiently moist soil, in sun or partial shade. They may be grown from seed or cuttings taken in early summer.

B.J. Both these plants grow and flower well in my area. Both are easy and trouble-free once established. *Gentiana verna* is another lovely species for the rock garden but not really for the beginner. *Gentiana sino-ornata* forms dense mats of procumbent stems and blooms very late; it requires acidic soil. Gentians are a group of plants that should be tried by every serious rock gardener.

T.C. The spring gentian (*Gentiana acaulis*) has grown for several years in a nursery bed containing a well-drained soil mix. They do not flower every year, but often enough to be encouraging. *Gentiana septemfida* flowers in the summer and can be relied upon to bloom every year.

A.P. *Gentiana acaulis* is the best of the long-lived spring gentians. Typical royal blue trumpets. Good in paving stones and limy soil. *Gentiana septemfida* needs adequate summer moisture if it is to flower well, but it is always a bit floppy. What about the acid-loving autumn species, such as *G. sino-ornata*?

P.K. Gentians are more easily grown here than is usually suspected. *Gentiana verna* likes a rich, moist soil in the sun, and the trumpet gentian thrives in a humusy, gritty loam where it can form large clumps

48

in time. The summer gentians (*G. septem-fida*) are easily grown in full sun or partial shade, as long as they have a good loamy soil.

G.S. To me, the gentians best illustrate the most delightful qualities of alpine plants: their smallness, their (often) large and colourful flowers. No other plants have the intensely blue flowers of many members of this genus. These two and *Gentiana sino-ornata* are widely grown here. Other species are too tall for the alpine garden but good for perennial beds. Some are more difficult to grow and are collectors' items.

Geranium spp

(cranesbill)

A genus of colourful spring- and summer-flowering plants with many hardy dwarf species that are suitable for the rock garden; these are not to be confused with florists' geraniums, which are pelargoniums, close relatives. *Geranium argenteum*, from the limestone

screes of Italy, forms silvery tufts with cuplike silver-pink blooms; *G. sanguineum*,* a European native, forms looser, more trailing mounds with strong pink flowers and attractive fall leaf colour. Well-drained, gritty, not overly rich soil is required. Propagate by root divison at almost any time of the year.

B.J. *Geranium sanguineum* and *G.s. lancastriense* will brighten up any rock garden. I have not tried *G. argenteum*, but others that grow well for me are *G. sub-caulescens* and *G. dalmaticum*, both superb small geraniums. For something different, try *G. sessiflorum nigra*, which has very tiny white flowers but interesting chocolate-brown leaves. This one is short-lived in my area but maintains its presence by self-sown seeds. Another, though larger, species to try is *G. renardii*; its

49

leaves and flowers are both quite unusual. All these plants will stand full sun but should not be allowed to become too dry.

T.C. The pink Dalmatian geranium (*Geranium dalmaticum*) and the magenta bloody cranesbill (*G. sanguineum*) both grow well and are fairly hardy here. I have not tried *G. argenteum* in Ottawa.

A.P. The species *Geranium argenteum* is very small – for a geranium – and has silver leaves.

P.K. Many geraniums are valuable rock garden plants for their lustrous foliage and glorious fall colour. One of the tiniest and choicest geraniums, *Geranium argenteum* is the silver geranium of the alps and grows best in a gritty loam in partial shade. *Geranium dalmaticum* is easily grown under many conditions.

G.S. *Geranium argenteum* is not grown here as often as are *G. cinereum* (especially the cultivar 'Ballerina'), *G. renardii*, *G. dalmaticum* and *G. sanguineum* (as well as several of its varieties and cultivars), all of which are small enough to fit well into the rock garden. *Geranium sanguineum* reseeds prolifically around the garden in our climate. There are a number of other larger geranium species that are often grown, but they are more suitable for a perennial border.

Globularia trichosantha

(globe daisy)

The globularias, natives chiefly of the Mediterranean region, include several creeping, mat-forming species. *Globularia trichosantha** is one of these; *G. cordifolia*, a dwarf species, is perhaps choicer. Both are characterized by mats of dark green rosettes, from which globelike flower heads arise in varying shades of blue. They want sun and a well-drained, gritty soil. Increase by seed, division or summer cuttings.

B.J. Have not grown this species. We have *Globularia nudicaulis* and *G. repens* in our scree. Neither is very floriferous,

but whether this is due to a less-than-ideal site or our climate, I could not say. The gardener with limited space could possibly use it to better advantage.

T.C. Several of the globe daisies have been grown here in the last few years. They all seem quite hardy and are useful for their later season of bloom.

A.P. Texturally useful. Stiff stems and blue heads make an unusual pattern. Seems to resent clay soil here.

P.K. Easily grown in scree or loam, the globe daisies are a delightful true-blue addition to the early summer garden. *Globularia trichosantha* forms a gradually expanding mat of evergreen rosettes, with blue powder puffs in May and June. *Globularia cordifolia* is a rapidly spreading mat.

G.S. Several species of *Globularia* are grown often in our area but are not well known to the general public. The round heads of soft blue flowers suggest a kinship to the daisy family, but they are in their own separate family.

Gypsophila repens

(baby's-breath)

The dwarf alpine species of this familiar plant are of a more compact, cushion-forming habit than the frothy annual or perennial gypsophilas usually associated with the bride's bouquet. *Gypsophila repens** is barely 6 inches high, with narrow, pale blue-green leaves and white or pinkish flowers in clusters. It is a native of the mountains of Europe and prefers a well-drained limy soil and full sun. It may be grown from seed or from cuttings taken from nonwoody shoots.

B.J. This is a fine plant for the beginner and grows very well in my area. The flowers of *Gypsophila repens* 'Rosea' are particularly pleasing, and *G. r. fratensis* also does well. *Gypsophila cerastioides* is a pleasant enough plant but possibly not as consistently hardy as *G. repens*.

T.C. While this is hardy in Ottawa, it has never produced the large mats I have seen in warmer climates.

A.P. A splendid carpet of grey grassy leaves and a cloud of white or pink (culti-var 'Rosea') flowers.

P.K. A fast-spreading mat that blooms heavily in early summer in any hot, dry exposure. Can overwhelm delicate alpines and self-sows moderately if conditions are too lush.

G.S. This low-spreading plant is a must in any rock garden or in crevices of rock walls. It is available locally, but we lose ours some winters, probably because they get too wet.

Iberis sempervirens

(evergreen candytuft)

A member of the prolific mustard family, iberis is, in the wild, native only to Europe, North Africa and western Asia. Many species are found in Spain, the ancient Iberia. *Iberis sempervirens** is a spreading, bushy subshrub with a woody stem, evergreen leaves and a covering of white flowers in late spring and early summer. All the candytufts require full sun and good soil drainage, and though they prefer limy soils, they can accept slight acidity. Propagate from nonwoody cuttings taken in summer.

B.J. *Iberis sempervirens* 'Little Gem' and 'Snowflake' are great plants for the rock garden in my area, 'Little Gem' being particularly popular with visitors to the botanical garden at St. John's; it looks very good hanging over a dry stone wall. We also have the tiny, low-growing *I. saxatilis* (syn. *I. petraea*) in our scree. All are hardy and bloom profusely but must have their flower heads cut off as soon as they fade.

T.C. Lightly trim off the old blooms as soon as flowering is finished, but try to avoid giving it a "sheared" look. This will make the shoots bush out and improve the next year's flowering.

A.P. If healthy and well looked after (good drainage, reasonable food, full sun), this is an excellent plant, strong enough in form and foliage to give "weight" to the rock garden, with the bonus of a fine late-spring display.

P.K. The common forms of candytuft are too vigorous and spreading for any but the largest rock gardens, but *Iberis saxatilis* is a tiny evergreen mat – barely an inch tall – with the same blindingly white flowers at the height of spring. Easily grown in sun or shade.

G.S. Another of the standards for the rock garden, but overused (see my comments under *Alyssum*). It is readily available from any garden shop; the less common compact forms ('Compacta' and 'Nana') are better.

Leontopodium alpinum

(edelweiss)

This native of the European Alps must be one of the best-known – or most notorious – alpines. It has, in the past at least, had the reputation of causing many mountainside tragedies, as incautious climbers lost their footing reaching to pluck its flowers. The true flowers are very small, surrounded by the familiar bracts, whose flannel-like greyness is said to become white when the plants inhabit a soil rich in lime. Good drainage and full sun are other requirements. Propagate from seed.

B.J. No doubt an interesting and even beautiful plant in its native habitat or in the hatband of a Swiss alpine guide, but decidedly ugly in cultivation. Though I have never seen a decent plant, beauty is in the eye of the beholder, so I may be doing it an injustice. In my area, *Leontopodium alpinum** starts growing very late in spring – just when you're sure it's dead. If you must grow it, give it well-drained soil in full sun.

T.C. To most people, this plant typifies the Alps. I hope that in its native habitat it puts on a better show than it does in Ottawa. Personally, I consider it a much overrated plant that I grow only because people expect to find it in the rock garden.

A.P. A dreary plant cut out of dingy flannel, whose romantic associations (and glutinous popular song) are not at all justified.

P.K. A short-lived tuffet for any sunny site with loam. There are more glamorous and longer-lived relatives of this in Asia worth pursuing.

G.S. Grey, woolly basal leaves and

52

bracts surrounding the tiny flowers make this a desirable and endearing, but not showy, plant. It is generally not long-lived in our climate unless given a very well-drained, sunny situation. It is better known in song than in real life.

Lewisia cotyledon

(lewisia)

The lewisias, members of the purslane family, are found exclusively in North America, inhabiting the Rockies in areas where there is excellent drainage and good winter snow cover. *Lewisia cotyledon,** from the mountains of northern California and southern Oregon, has basal rosettes of fleshy evergreen leaves and copious flowers in shades of pink that appear in spring. The lewisias are highly prized in the rock garden but are considered difficult to maintain in health; they are, however, comparatively easy to start from seed. A fairly rich soil mix and some shade are required.

B.J. Lewisias are very difficult to grow in my area, usually succumbing to summer rot. We are still working on this problem, and it is quite possible that some species would flourish here on a north-facing wall. (But first we have to get our north-facing wall.)

T.C. A genus that has a reputation for being very difficult; I have had considerable success with it, and almost all of the losses have been due to theft. Providing you plant it in very well-drained soil or in a crack between two rocks so that water cannot lie on the crown, this plant should thrive. Seed germinates well if you freeze it for 30 days before sowing.

A.P. A beautiful westerner best in wall crevices, to prevent water rotting the rosettes. Colour and texture not easy to associate with commoner things.

P.K. This aristocrat of alpines is invaluable year-round for its lustrous, succulent rosettes. The flowers are gorgeous and irresistible over a long

season in spring here. It thrives on rich scree or in a crevice – growing best, perhaps, in partial shade.

G.S. This and most of the other species of this genus, especially our native *Lewisia rediviva* and *L. tweedyi*, are among the choicest of alpine plants. They are particularly good for crevices in rocks or walls and are one of my favourite groups of rock garden plants. They deserve to be more widely grown.

Mentha requienii

(Corsican mint)

The mints are a large genus of aromatic herbs native to northern Eurasia and North America. *Mentha requienii,** Corsican mint, is the smallest of them all, a miniature creeper forming absolutely flat mats and the only species suited to the rock garden. It is especially useful between paving stones but needs moisture and some shade. Propagate by division   53 or root cuttings.

B.J. I have not seen this plant growing in my area.

T.C. This is surely the smallest of all rock garden plants but is unquestionably a mint. Just stroke your fingers over the soft green mat of leaves and you will be in no doubt. I have grown this tiny plant in my own garden for almost 15 years, and I am still not sure if it is hardy or if it comes up each spring from self-sown seed. It seems to prefer a site that is shaded from direct midday sun and also has some moisture.

A.P. *Mentha requienii* is the tiniest mint of all. It produces pinhead-sized leaves and flowers with an extraordinarily strong smell of water mint. Paving cracks make an ideal home for this plant, but it won't take heavy wear.

P.K. This has proven perfectly perennial in a moist, shady bank where one can hardly resist sniffing the heady peppermint odour.

G.S. Spreads readily (too readily) in our area, in wet soils in sunny locations, forming pale green, peppermint-scented carpets with tiny pale purple flowers in summer. Good to pinch and sniff or to use between paving stones, where it will withstand some foot traffic and release a pleasant scent.

Papaver alpinum

(alpine poppy)

The alpine poppy is a valuable plant for the rock garden, attractive with its mass of grey-green, deeply segmented leaves and its delicate flowers in many shades. It stands 6 to 8 inches tall, with blooms throughout the summer. A well-drained but slightly moist, not-too-rich limy soil suits it well, with either full sun or semi-shade.

B.J. This dainty little poppy grows well in my area. Though short-lived, it maintains its presence by self-sowing and, in this way, travels around the garden. It would be prudent to purchase and scatter new seed every few years. Full sun and good air circulation appear to be a must for this plant here. *Papaver radicatum* is a native of Labrador and should be tried if ever the seeds come your way. It produces

54

glorious sulphur yellow flowers on short, wiry stems.

T.C. Sow poppies where they are to flower; they don't like being transplanted. *Papaver alpinum** is not usually very persistent, but it will self-seed. It is generally only available in mixed colours, but there are often subspecies offered in the seed exchanges that are single-coloured. One of the nicest I have grown was *P. a. burseri* with lemon yellow flowers.

A.P. Elegant greyish tufts with fleeting flowers in a range of soft colours. Should be encouraged to self-seed.

P.K. This delightful, delicate poppy carries its many coloured, fragrant flowers over a filigreed mound of foliage. Rarely lives more than two years here, self-sowing sparingly in cool scree soil. A standard, almost indispensable. Easily grown from seed.

G.S. This and several other low-growing species of poppies are excellent for the rock garden and are commonly raised in the Vancouver area. The dissected, often grey foliage makes a nice foil for the very large, but delicate, flowers. Avoid the taller species in small rock gardens. They are relatively easy to grow from seed but are usually short-lived perennials.

Penstemon spp

(beard tongue)

The penstemons are almost entirely natives of North America, and most are to be found on the high plains, foothills and western mountain ranges. Among them are many species, such as *Penstemon newberryi*,* that are suitable for rock garden cultivation. They are not considered easy plants, but they are sufficiently intriguing to have had a society founded for their study. Their profuse summer display of tubular, snapdragonlike flowers is very rewarding, and most species bloom after much else in the rock garden is finished. They like a lean soil in full sun and do not appreciate being planted too close to their neighbours. Grow from seed.

B.J. I believe this genus has great potential in my area. There are so many beautiful penstemons that should be tried here.

T.C. Beard tongues range in size from a couple of inches to over 6 feet. A number of species do not thrive in the hot, muggy summers of the east, but of the many that I have grown, one I would recommend most strongly is *Penstemon pinifolius*. This has fine feathery foliage and bright red tubular flowers on 12-inch stems. Plants have survived for at least five years in a raised trough garden. *Penstemon hirsutus pygmaeus* and *P. teucrioides* are a couple of dwarf forms (only 1 inch tall in leaf) that have also survived for several years here. Both are spring-flowering, and the first continues to bloom for most of the summer.

A.P. All the dwarf Rocky Mountain penstemons are valuable rock garden shrublets and useful to the limit of their hardiness.

P.K. Penstemons are ideally suited to 55

our climate, and over 100 kinds, from shrubby *Penstemon dasantheras* to the mat-forming *P. caespitosi*, are being grown locally. *Penstemon alpinus*, Rocky Mountain penstemon, a medium-size species native to the Front Range of the Colorado Rockies, carries a dense spike of true-blue flowers and adapts well to a wide variety of garden conditions.

G.S. A huge genus of predominantly western North American species, they produce dozens of excellent low plants with large flowers in a broad range of colours from white through pink, blue, purple and brilliant orange and red. Most require a very sunny spot with excellent drainage here on the wet B.C. coast. Some are tall and should be used in the perennial border.

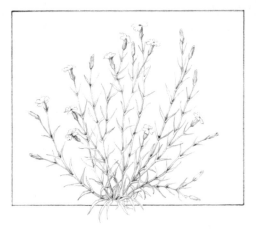

Petrorhagia saxifraga

formerly Tunica saxifraga
(saxifrage pink)

This is a small genus of low-growing, tufted and spreading plants, which is a member of the pink family and a native of Eurasia. The leaves are narrow and tiny, the flowers also tiny and in the pink to lilac range. Saxifrage pink is easily grown in ordinary garden soil and is propagated by seed or by root division.

B.J. I do not know of anyone who has tried to grow *Petrorhagia saxifraga** in my area—a situation that should be rectified.

T.C. A plant that is worth growing, since it blooms in the summer. The individual pink flowers are small, but en masse, they create a misty effect that is especially striking when used behind some of the mound type of bellflowers.

A.P. Of the *Gypsophila repens* and *Saponaria ocymoides* ilk; clouds of little pink or white flowers. Full sun, with limy well-drained soil.

P.K. A symmetrical mound of baby's-breath blossoms for much of the summer, June to August. Useful for its airy effect

and as a light cover over bulbs. Double-flowered pink and white forms are preferable for small rock gardens, since the single form can become a nuisance by aggressively self-sowing.

G.S. Looks like a slender, wiry-stemmed gypsophila. Good for its cloud-like masses of small pink flowers in summer and autumn.

Phlox subulata

(moss pink)

Moss pink, an excellent carpeting plant with deep cerise blossoms, is a native of eastern North America, and many garden varieties have been developed in a wide range of pinks, blues and whites. *Phlox subulata** forms a dense mat, rooting along its stems; the foliage is evergreen and prickly, and the flowers grow in clusters. Other species have a more trailing habit. They do well in a sandy, stony soil with adequate warmth and moisture. Grow from cuttings or by root division.

B.J. This plant, in many shades, has been thriving in my area for decades, an ideal beginner's plant. Equally hardy but more compact is *Phlox douglasii. Phlox nivalis* and *P. borealis* also do quite well but require more attention to keep them alive. *Phlox stolonifera* 'Blue Ridge' is a superb plant for light shade and a woodsy soil. Phlox hate our heavy wet snow, and as soon as it has melted, they must be fluffed up in order to dry out and ward off rot.

T.C. Along with *Arabis* and *Aubrieta*, this genus is one of the mainstays of the spring rock garden. It should be lightly sheared after flowering to remove the old blossoms and encourage new growth. Some varieties of low-growing phlox will flower again in the fall.

A.P. Wonderful range of colours in late spring, in such a quantity as to hide the foliage entirely. Good drainage is essential, but clay is not rejected. Easy and dependable.

P.K. Durable when given sufficient moisture and a great contributor to the spring fling of colour. Dwarf selections available for smaller gardens include 'Schneewittchen' and 'Ronsdorf Beauty.'

G.S. Care-free and easy to grow in sunny, well-drained locations, but over-used locally. There are many other things much better. Best used in small clumps, rather than in great drifts. Colour forms other than the usual magenta are more pleasing alongside most rockery plants.

Potentilla tridentata

(three-toothed cinquefoil)

Growing widely throughout the north temperate and subarctic zones, potentil-las, members of the rose family, include shrubs and perennials as well as alpines. Many species are desirable for the rock garden. *Potentilla tridentata,** found in Greenland and much of the eastern United States and Canada, is a shiny evergreen subshrub with clusters of white blossoms; the foliage turns brilliant red in the fall. Other species have golden or apricot-coloured flowers. Propagate from seed or by division.

B.J. A common little native plant that flourishes here in gritty, nutrient-poor soil in full sun. Also try *Potentilla verna nana, P. megalantha* 'Take,' *P. villosa, P. × 'Tonquei' and P. nitida.* The latter is the aristocrat of the genus. It should be grown in a scree in full sun and does better under frugal conditions, so be careful not to overfeed it. It's an absolute beauty if you can get it and provide it with what it wants.

T.C. I have seen this plant growing wild   57

from northern Ontario to North Carolina, on rocky outcrops and bluffs where little else will grow. In Ottawa, it has been growing for almost 20 years and flowers regularly. Do not plant in rich soil or feed during the growing season. *Potentilla verna nana*, the dwarf spring cinquefoil, displays bright yellow flowers in early spring and usually blooms again in late summer and fall. It forms a green carpet less than 1 inch tall when not in flower.

P.K. Can become a pest, spreading by underground runners. Excellent fall colour. Can scorch in sunny winters.

G.S. Another large genus with many very good plants, in a wide range of colours and with pleasant foliage textures. *Potentilla tridentata* is fairly commonly grown here. It has white flowers raised above dark green, toothed leaves; easy to grow. One could specialize and fill a rock garden with this genus alone. This species does spread and could be a bit invasive in a small rock garden, but it can be trimmed back easily. It is sometimes used in the Vancouver area as a ground cover.

Primula spp

(primrose)

This enormous genus embraces such a wide assortment of plants that, for the sake of easier orientation, they have been grouped into 20 sections. The section *Auricula* comprises *Primula auricula** and a number of other related species that are suitable for the rock garden. Native to the European Alps, *P. auricula* forms groups of rosettes and clustered yellow blossoms in rock crevices. This particular species appreciates sun and limy, humus-rich soil; other primroses require some shade. All primulas may be grown from seed or by division of older clumps.

B.J. This genus has tremendous potential in my area, and we have at present approximately 150 species under trial. They respond to our cool, damp climate, but many are more appropriately

grown in the woodland bed. The smaller species, especially those of the *Farinosa* section, are prone to root damage, which is caused by frost heave. A nice one for a stone wall or rock crevice is *Primula marginata* (of the *Auricula* section). Its woody stems must be kept dry and well circulated with air. Also try *P. pubescens*, especially *P.p. alba*, if you get the chance. The latter makes an excellent potted plant for the alpine house or cold frame.

T.C. There is a multitude of primroses that can be grown in the rock garden, but most of them are shade lovers and need a woodsy type of soil. The group known as *juliae* hybrids are the easiest. These come in a great range of colours and include the best-known primrose of all, 'Wanda.' Keep an eye open for discoloured foliage in the summer; mites are very attracted to primroses and cause the foliage to yellow rapidly. In full sun and in alkaline soils, the *Auricula* section will thrive.

A.P. Primroses need a chapter entirely to themselves: all small primulas are worth growing. Most need adequate moisture. Especially easy are the 'Wanda' group and *Primula sieboldii. Primula vulgaris/sibthorpii* need half shade, while *P. veris* is happy in full sun.

P.K. The best for our climate are the evergreen, clump-forming species of the *Auricula* section. *Primula sieboldii* can form large mats in a cool, shady garden. Most other primulas require frequent irrigation or even a bog treatment to thrive here.

G.S. One of the most widely grown groups of alpine plants in the Vancouver area, from very dwarf, early (and easy) *Primula juliae* cultivars and larger *P. denticulata* to *P. auricula*, short-lived but showy *P. polyanthus* and *P. vialii* and moisture-loving *candelabra* species. If the many different species are grown, they give a long season of flowering, from late winter through early summer. Many are available locally from plants or seed, and some reseed readily once established in the garden. There are many others for the specialist or for a cool greenhouse culture.

Pulsatilla vulgaris

(pasque flower)

An anemone-like plant of the buttercup family (often included in the genus *Anemone* as *Anemone pulsatilla*), the pasque flower is a dramatic and valuable inhabitant of the rock garden. The leaves are feathery and appear in early spring at the same time as the blue or reddish purple bell-shaped flowers; in due course, the blooms are replaced by plumy seed heads. They need porous soil with good drainage and full sun. Propagation is by seed.

B.J. *Pulsatilla vulgaris** is an excellent plant for my area. Larger pulsatillas do not move well, so place them in your garden as large seedlings. The seed heads, too, are attractive, and by leaving them to disintegrate on the stalk, you may have the added bonus of the occasional young plant popping up later in the most unlikely places. Also try *P. alpina sulphurea*, which is equally desirable but has yellow flowers. If you are very keen and don't despair too easily, you should also try *P. vernalis*

from the European Alps. It really hates our wet snow, but in those springs when it does manage to flower, it is really worth having.

T.C. Do not be in a hurry to cut off the seed heads. The silky seeds are almost as attractive as the flowers.

A.P. These plants have exquisite purple cups with golden stamens in a cloud of young foliage. White, pink and near-red forms exist – but some lose their usual elegant look by being too tall. Good seed heads. Lime; full sun.

P.K. Its self-sown seedlings can completely overwhelm a garden, but, oh, how charming the flowers are in early spring.

G.S. *Pulsatilla vulgaris* and several others are among my favourites for rock gardens. The large flowers are some of the earliest out in winter (if it is mild) or in early spring and are pretty from the time the soft fuzzy buds emerge, through flowering, to the fernlike foliage of 59 summer and the plumes of seeds. Easy to grow and long-lasting. Several European and North American species have been cultivated locally.

Sagina subulata

(pearlwort)

A genus of the pink family, *Sagina* has only a few species, all from the north temperate zone and often of a tufted or matted habit. *Sagina subulata*,* a native of Corsica, has mosslike foliage and a profusion of minute white flowers. It prefers a rich, moist soil and semi-shade. Propagate by division.

B.J. The naming of this and similar plants is extremely confusing. For those who do not specialize in plant taxonomy, this plant seems little different from *Arenaria verna caespitosa*. As rock garden subjects, saginas really don't warrant all this mental exercise.

T.C. Closely related to *Arenaria* but much more invasive, they are useful as ground covers on a walkway.

A.P. Similar to *Arenaria verna*. A golden form also exists. Good as a ground cover and in association with the smallest spring bulbs.

P.K. Most winters knock it back a bit, but it usually recovers by summer's end. Grow it in moist, partly shaded loam.

G.S. Good as a very low-growing ground cover but needs to be kept

60

trimmed back as it may be invasive here. The golden-leaved forms are very attractive on our dull rainy days. Good for use in rock crevices and for softening the edges of rocks.

Saponaria ocymoides

(soapwort)

This European species of *Saponaria*, another member of the prolific pink family, has a more trailing habit than some of its sister species and is especially effective in rock walls. The leaves are dark green, the profuse flowers a reddish pink. *Saponaria ocymoides** flourishes in full sun and porous, sandy soil. It may be increased by division, cuttings or seed.

B.J. Another superb plant for the beginner, and though it is somewhat rampant, common and easily grown from seed, I cannot imagine a stone wall or rock garden without it. Give it a hard shearing after flowering so that its energy is not wasted on making seed and it remains compact and floriferous. Also try the more compact *Saponaria* × *olivana* and *S. lutea*. These two are more of a challenge but grow well for us in the scree or other very well-drained sites in full sun. The latter plants are good for those gardeners with little space.

T.C. Very easy to raise from seed, this is a most useful plant since it blooms in mid- to late summer when little else in the

rock garden is in flower. It has a trailing habit and should be planted so that it can cascade over a rock face.

A.P. Good, delicate spreader, with small leaves and pink flowers. Associates well with dianthus and hangs contentedly over walls.

P.K. The typical form is somewhat invasive but extremely durable in hot spots. *Saponaria ocymoides* 'Rubra Compacta' is a more restrained companion in the rock garden, however, and *S. pumilio* is a superb cushion.

G.S. A low, wide-spreading perennial covered with pink flowers in spring and a few later in the season. It is common here and easy to grow.

Saxifraga spp

(saxifrage, rockfoil)

Although their name is derived from two Latin words meaning "to break rock," saxifrages are not, in fact, responsible for the minute rock cracks and crevices they seem to prefer. This is an enormous genus with species of widely varying habits; *Saxifraga* is roughly divided between encrusted types, with lime deposits on the edges of the leaves, and mossy types, which form dense cushions and are considered more difficult to grow. *Saxifraga aizoon* (silver saxifrage) belongs to the first group, with rosettes of silvery lime-encrusted leaves and sprays of white flowers in the spring. Most saxifrages thrive in semi-shaded locations and may be propagated by division or by seed.

B.J. Another extensive group with great potential. A good large species is *Saxifraga cotyledon* caterhamensis*. The miniature London pride, *S. umbrosa primuloides*, does well but requires a little more moisture and shade. Try also *S. aizoon* and *S. lingulata*. The native *S. oppositifolia* requires some fussing and is best left alone by the beginner. The mossy-type saxifrages such as *S. caespitosa grandiflora*, *S.* 'Elf,' *S.* 'Glassel

Crimson' and *S.* 'Nona Megrory' require a cool, shady site. The cushion-type *S. burseriana* and *S. b. sulphurea* grow for us but require a scree or an equally well-drained site. They flower very early and can be caught by late snow showers.

T.C. During the 20-plus years that I have been rock gardening in Ottawa, I must have tried several dozen different "Saxies." Few of them are still with me. In part, this is because I didn't always give them the well-drained scree conditions that many prefer. Most have disappeared during the summer doldrums, when humidity is high and temperatures hover in the 90s. Some have survived in spite of everything. The mossy type, with its thin bright green leaves, *Saxifraga rosea* has grown for several years in a location where a rock shades it from the midday sun; its single flowers are bright pink. The 61 encrusted types, with rosettes of leaves often silvery or whitish in colour – among others, *S. callosa* 'Albertii' and *S. cotyledon icelandica* – have also done well. Other types such as *S. umbrosa primuloides* 'Elliott,' a miniature form of London pride, grew and flowered for five or six years.

A.P. A vast number of species varying from the very difficult to the very easy. Mossy types give good carpets of foliage and small sprays of pink flowers. *Saxifraga hypnoides* is only 6 inches high, while *S. umbrosa* is a London pride whose form *S. u. primuloides* is of better rock garden size. As regards the wonderful rosette-forming types such as 'Tumbling Waters,' I know nothing of their cultivation in North America.

P.K. The porophyllums begin the season and perform best in gritty, shaded crevices. The silver saxifrages take a little more sun and add to the glory of the May garden. They can sunburn in midsummer, if put in too bright an exposure.

G.S. A huge genus of mostly alpine and high-elevation plants, ranging from the easy-to-grow, such as *Saxifraga umbrosa* (London pride), to many very difficult species. A large number of these are better left to the avid alpine enthusiast or grown in a cool greenhouse, as winter wetness is a problem in the Vancouver area. Many may be bought locally as plants or grown from seed.

Sedum spp

(stonecrop)

Another bewilderingly large genus, *Sedum* has species in a wide range of appearances and habits. Beware of any that have a reputation for aggressiveness. Widely distributed over the northern hemisphere, they are creeping, mat-forming plants, frequently succulent, their leaves often in spirals and their flowers in clusters along the upper sides of coiled branches. Because the genus is so extensive, it is organized into several groups;

the largest, a subgenus named, confusingly, *Sedum*, contains many of the hardy, low carpeting plants suitable to the rock garden. Among these are two summer-flowering species, *S. spurium,* * with purplish blooms and dark green leaves, and *S. dasyphyllum*, forming a mat of blue-grey leaves and pink blossoms. Sedums need a well-drained soil and full sun; propagate by seed, cuttings or division.

B.J. Sedums are one of the mainstays of the beginner's rock garden, but not all species are as easy or desirable as we may wish. *Sedum album* planted against *S. a.* 'Chloraticum' is effective and easy. *Sedum acre* can be invasive, but I like its flash of yellow stars and have no trouble controlling it. *Sedum spurium, S. kamtschaticum* and *S. k.* 'Variegatum' are all easy to grow and as tough as nails. *Sedum ewersii, S. sieboldii* and *S. cauticola* are all temperamental in our climate, requiring extra thought and attention to do well. *Sedum anglicum*, unfortunately, does not survive our winters. *Sedum spathuli-*

folium 'Casa Blanca' will not survive in our rock garden but grows well in a mixture of sand and peat in the light shade of our peat beds. Try *S. middendorfianum* if you get the chance.

T.C. Some stonecrops should be found in every rock garden; others should not be in any. Stay away from the golden stonecrop (*Sedum acre*), *S. nevii* and *S. album*. They are all brittle, and every piece will root and make a new plant. Good guys include Siebold's stonecrop (*S. sieboldii*), with grey leaves that trail slowly over a rock face, and *S. spathulifolium* 'Casa Blanca' (often listed in catalogues as 'Capa Blanca'), which has little tight rosettes of grey leaves. One of my favourites is *S. sempervivoides*, the houseleek stonecrop. This is a biennial, and after flowering, it sets seeds and dies. The seed will usually germinate the following spring, however, if allowed to fall around the parent. Sow this two years running to get some plants flowering each year.

A.P. The smaller sedums are many; fine foliage often added to late-season flower. Especially good are *Sedum spathulifolium*, *S. rosea* and *S. sieboldii* 'Variegatum.' Avoid *S. acre* as too weedy for rock gardens. All need good drainage but reasonable moisture in spite of succulent appearance.

P.K. Beware of *Sedum album*, *S. acre* and even the colourful selections of *S. spurium*, which can easily overwhelm. Noninvasive species, whose colourful addition to the late-summer garden is often undervalued, include *S. ewersii*, *S. sieboldii* and *S. tatarinowii*.

G.S. Good and very easy group of plants for the beginner who has full sun and a well-drained situation. Some are invasive and should be thinned out every few years. Don't plant them near smaller, slow-growing plants that may get crowded out by the sedums. There is a wide range of textures and colours of succulent leaves and rather showy flowers. Most are suitable for the rock garden, but a few, such as *Sedum spectabile*, are large enough that they are better grown in the perennial border.

Sempervivum spp

(houseleek)

The name, meaning "always living," epitomizes the hardiness and tenacity of these interesting plants. They show a great diversity of form and colour, and several species grow together most attractively in the rock garden. Their stemless, succulent, greyish leaves in dense rosettes are most familiar in the very commonly grown *Sempervivum tectorum*, hen and chickens, or roof houseleek (from its habit of nestling happily in European country thatches), and in the more delicate *S. arachnoideum*, which spins weblike hairs across its globe-shaped rosettes. Bracted stalks arising from leaf rosettes bear clusters of flowers in shades of yellow, red or purple. A light well-drained soil will suffice for the sempervivums, and they can take full sun. Propagate by seed or by the offsets that they produce so readily.

B.J. There are so many houseleeks that   63

the problem lies in choosing which to grow. Better to keep to just a few of the more obviously different ones, such as *Sempervivum arachnoideum stanfieldii, S. fauconnettii, S. hookeri, S. atropurpureum, S.* 'Reginald Malby,' *S. engels rubrum* and *S.* 'Dick Hayward.' They are ideal for stone walls, troughs and rock crevices. To grow them in the slight depression at the top of large rocks, first paint the indentation with molasses, then add your soil mixture and press it down so that it is stuck to the rock by the molasses; then, carefully poke in the small offsets of your favourite sempervivums. This trick works remarkably well for us, but many people think we are just pulling their leg.

T.C. One could make an entire garden using nothing but houseleeks. There are several hundred different ones, varying in size from the tiny *Sempervivum arachnoideum*, the cobweb houseleek, to some of the named forms with rosettes over 6 inches across. Not generally thought of as flowering plants, a large clump of "semps" in bloom is definitely eye-catching.

A.P. All species and cultivars are admirable for rock crevices, trough culture and even growing on moist tile roofs (hence the English common name "Welcome Home Husband However Drunk You Be").

P.K. So easily grown that they're taken almost for granted, houseleeks are often relegated to hot dry corners where they may burn and look unsightly at the height of summer heat. *Sempervivum arachnoideum* is the gem of the genus for its fascinating cobwebby rosettes and its pink flowers. It thrives even in hot crevices. *Sempervivum ciliosum* in its various forms offers eyelashed leaves of comparable beauty and vivid yellow flowers. Many of the houseleeks are now segregated in the genus *Jovibarba*, including the roly-poly *J. sobolifera* (which can become a pest among choice miniatures) and *J. heuffelii*.

G.S. Excellent for rock crevices in hot, sunny places and often used in combination with the sedums. A few species are grown commonly; many others are not often seen. The cobwebby types are especially pleasing.

Silene spp

(catchfly, moss campion)

Another genus under the umbrella of the pink family, *Silene* has a great number of species throughout the world, some perennial, some annual, and all of varying degrees of hardiness. Comparatively few are in cultivation. *Silene acaulis,** a native of North America, is one of these, a small tufted plant with purplish flowers appearing throughout the summer. Sun and well-drained soil are needed, and the plants may be increased by seed, division or cuttings.

B.J. The little native *Silene acaulis* is difficult to grow well and not recommended for the beginner. *Silene schafta* blooms late, and though short-lived with us, it is very easy and quick to grow from seed, so it is useful for the new rock gardener. The biennial *S. armeria* is possibly too tall for the average home rock garden;

nonetheless, it is easily propagated from seed and produces large heads of crimson flowers. No rock garden should be without the starry white flowers of *S. alpestris*. It is easy to grow in a scree or other open, well-drained soil. Propagates easily from seed. Cut off the multitude of flower stalks as soon as the blooms fade.

T.C. This plant gets its common name from the tiny sticky hairs on the calyx that trap small flies. None of the botanists I have spoken to can give me any good explanation of why silenes are able to do this. It does not seem to benefit them in any way. The moss campion (*Silene acaulis*) grows at high altitudes over much of the northern hemisphere. This is one plant that grew well in Ottawa and, even more remarkably, transplanted well when mature. It forms a low green hummock studded with bright pink, starry flowers in spring. One of my favourite silenes is the little annual weed *S. armeria*. This pops up in a different place each year, and the bright magenta flowers are always eye-catching, so it is easy to weed out if it invades a more desirable plant. There are usually a few clumps of it to bloom into late summer.

A.P. *Silene acaulis* is the lovely moss pink or moss campion of the Far North. Does wonderfully on Baffin Island but apt to flower less well in the more comfortable south. *Silene colorata* is a useful pink annual for sowing around small bulbs to create an interesting summer combination.

P.K. With its green mat and airy white flowers, *Silene alpestris flore-pleno* is charming and durable. We have not succeeded yet with the alluring *S. californica* and *S. petersonii*.

G.S. *Silene* has many useful species for the rock garden, but some are weedy and others are too tall and better used in a perennial border. The best ones, including *S. acaulis*, *S. caroliniana* and *S. hookeri*, need a very sunny location in well-drained, relatively poor soil to be at their healthiest. Many taller species such as the red-flowered *S. virginica*, *S. laciniata* and *S. californica* are good in larger gardens.

Thymus spp

(thyme)

This aromatic genus, belonging to the mint family, is native mainly to the Mediterranean region and is well known in some forms as a kitchen herb, in others as a rock garden plant. Among the latter, *Thymus serpyllum*,* mother-of-thyme, is a spreader with small leaves and tiny purplish flowers; *T. pseudolanuginosus*, woolly thyme, makes neater, greyish carpets in paving cracks, with pink flowers in summer. They do well in limy soils in full sun and may be grown from seed or by division or cuttings.

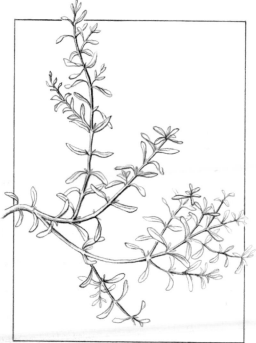

B.J. Useful plants for carpeting over certain bulbs or between patio stones and similar sites. We have the very prostrate *Thymus serpyllum angustifolium* and the white-flowered *T. s.* 'Montanus Albus,' 65

which, however, looks dirty when it fades. For greyish foliage and mauve flowers, try *T. pseudolanuginosus* or, better still, *T. l. hirsutus doerfleri.*

T.C. When I first started renovating the rock garden in Ottawa, every time I needed space for some new planting, I would dig out more of the carpets of thyme. I was quite pleased with the way the renovation was progressing until one day I overheard two visitors talking: "You know, they have spoiled this garden since they took all that pink stuff out." There are a large number of thymes that can be grown, each with a slightly different scent. The only one I have not been successful with is the variegated form of the creeping thyme, *Thymus serpyllum* 'Silver Queen.' For some reason, this does not seem as hardy as other clones.

A.P. All the creeping thymes are valuable ground covers, not getting above a couple of inches high. Good with dwarf bulbs. *Thymus pseudolanuginosus* is grey and, in a carpet, contrasts well with the *T. serpyllum* types.

P.K. Extremely durable and useful, the more widely grown species such as *Thymus serpyllum* and *T. pseudolanuginosus* can overrun a small garden but are good along paths or between flagstones. Choice plants for cushions include *T. serpyllum* 'Minus,' *T. necefii* and *T. cilicius.*

G.S. This genus of familiar species is a vital part of the alpine garden, forming soft, low mats covered with white, mauve, pink or purple flowers. Many different species and forms are available locally and are easy to grow. Some need to be trimmed back or dug and divided every few years to keep them from growing over other more slowly growing plants.

Veronica spp

(speedwell)

This genus is widespread and very diverse in its species, which range from sizable shrubs (sometimes assigned to the genus *Hebe*) to the low-growing, mat-forming plants associated with the rock garden. Among the latter are *Veronica repens,** a tiny creeper from Corsica with pale blue or whitish flowers, which appreciates moist soil and partial shade; and the taller *V. incana*, from northern Asia, with striking silver-grey leaves and spikes of blue-violet blooms, which requires a dryish, well-drained soil. All may be increased by division.

B.J. The tiny *Veronica repens* grows well in our area but travels around and can burn out badly in hot weather. If you have the space, *V. incana* and *V. teucrium* are useful, provided they are in fairly nutrient-poor soil. *Veronica fruticulosa* is not hardy with us. I particularly like *V. stelleri* from Japan, however, and recommend it if you can get reliable seed.

T.C. Many of the speedwells can be invasive weeds, so if you are growing them from seed, try them in a less vital part of the garden first. The woolly speedwell, *Veronica incana*, and its pink form, 'Rosea,' provide a good backdrop for other low plants, even when not in flower. The stiff, upright grey foliage is particularly effective behind bright red or yellow flowers.

A.P. *Veronica incana* is good for grey foliage and 1-foot blue spikes, while *V. prostrata* is rather lower and a more constant flowerer (there are a number of named forms). *Veronica caespitosa* is a much more specialized rock garden plant from the mountains of eastern Europe.

P.K. *Veronica prostrata* is really the best, although several Turkish species recently introduced are showing great promise. Good as cover for bulbs and easy to grow.

G.S. A very large genus of everything from weeds to desirable rock garden plants and taller herbaceous perennials. Many small ones suitable for the rock garden are easy to obtain and grow here, including *Veronica incana* and *V. prostrata*. They all bring various shades of blue to the garden.

Viola spp

(violet)

This is another familiar genus whose species are frequently invasive and should therefore be chosen with care. Two native North American species are *Viola labradorica*,* the Labrador violet, existing in the wild from southern parts of the Canadian eastern Arctic to eastern Greenland, and *V. pedata*, the bird's-foot violet, of the eastern United States, a particularly choice plant to grow with its violet-mauve flowers. Dryish soil and semi-shade are required. Some forms of violet are self-sowing or may be grown from seed; others spread by runners, and yet others may be increased by division or cuttings.

B.J. I have little knowledge of choicer violas suitable for my area – no doubt I should do something about this. The common and much-loved *Viola tricolor*, with its multitude of colour variants, can produce very floriferous, lovely, compact plants in my gravel driveway, so it might be a good idea to try it in a frugal mixture in the rock garden.

T.C. All the books on alpine plants tell me that there are many wonderful violets just waiting to be grown in my rock garden. Experience has shown me a different side. With the possible exception of the Labrador violet, all have proved to be

either fleeting visitors or persistent pests. The two worst weeds in the rock garden at the Central Experimental Farm are the bulbous Star of Bethlehem (*Ornithogalum umbellatum*) and Johnny-jump-ups (*Viola* spp). The Labrador violet (*V. labradorica*), which has very attractive purplish foliage and small blue flowers, seemed to be very well behaved for the first two years but is now starting to pop up in unexpected places, either from seed or by runner – I suspect the latter. Being a shade lover, it is unlikely to colonize a very large area.

A.P. Some violets are rather aggressive for the specialist rock garden, but as long as it is ensured that seedlings do not swamp choice neighbours, all are useful. Most will take half shade. *Viola labradorica* has purple foliage; *V. septentrionalis* is the big-flowered blue and white Confederate violet.

P.K. Violets are prone to becoming ineradicable weeds in shady rock gardens, but the many wild relatives of the pansy are indispensable in cool rock work. *Viola* 67 *corsica* blooms through much of the winter, spring and fall; *V. cornuta* is another long-flowering plant, but it can also become invasive.

G.S. Many good and easy species, frequently grown here. *Viola labradorica* is the one most often seen, but it is quite weedy, popping up all over our gardens. One of my favourites, but not very common, is *V. saxatilis aetolica* with its bright yellow flowers. *Viola tricolor* and *V. cornuta* in their wild forms are common and easy, but several of the named selections are better. More difficult but very choice is *V. pedata* (bird's-foot violet), from the east.

Bulbs

(including Corms, Rhizomes and Tubers)

Despite the beauty of their early spring flowers and the linear foliage that contrasts so well with the cushions and mats of the other plants, bulbs present a few problems in the small rock garden. The larger ones are not only out of scale with their neighbours, but their leaves must be left undisturbed for a long period after blooming in order to nourish the bulbs, becoming increasingly unsightly in the process. Other bulbs require drying out in the summer when the rest of the garden needs moisture. And it may prove difficult to keep the spreading types under control. However, the smaller early-blooming bulbs that associate well with rocks – a setting in which they receive good drainage, protection from wind and the benefit of spring sunshine – are the ones to use. Plant them where they can easily be seen and where they show to best advantage.

Allium karataviense; A. moly

(ornamental onions)

An enormous genus of mostly onion-scented plants, including all the well-known edible forms and the garden ornamentals, alliums are found chiefly in the northern hemisphere and vary in height from a few inches to several feet. The flowers, more or less globe-shaped heads in a wide array of sizes, may be dense or airy in appearance and range from white through pink, rose red, blue and yellow. In many species, the flower heads produce bulbils, which provide an easy method of propagation. Leaves are typically hollow, sometimes flat. A generally hardy and fascinating tribe, alliums are a nice addition to many areas of a garden. Among the low-growing species suitable for the rock garden are *Allium karataviense,** a spring bloomer from Turkestan – though its wide, flat leaves and large grey-lavender heads may make it too dramatic for a small rock garden – and *A. moly*, which is somewhat taller, but more delicate, with its yellow flower heads appearing later in the season. Plant bulbs in the fall in a sunny position, where there is well-drained, gravelly loam.

B.J. Both will grow well in my area, though the former may prove a little large for the average home rock garden. Alliums show great potential for Newfoundland, and there should be many more species tried here. Among others, we have *Allium amabile, A. splendens, A. macranthum, A. sikkimense* and *A. cernuum*. The latter self-seeds freely, but unwanted ones can be given as gifts to other rock gardeners or are easily weeded out. All these alliums respond to loose, well-drained soil with a fair amount of well-rotted leaf mould mixed in.

T.C. *Allium karataviense* has not proved to be long-lasting in Ottawa, and while the large leaves are arresting, the flower is not very showy. The golden garlic, *A. moly*, is the reverse: the flowers are most attractive, and the plants will self-seed and even become a bit of a pest. One advantage of the golden garlic is that it flowers in summer, when most of the other onions are finished.

A.P. There are wonderful leaves on *Allium karataviense. Allium moly* is rather

weedy for the rock garden. Much better-behaved are *A. cernuum*, *A. cyaneum*, *A. narcissiflorum*, *A. ostrowskianum* and *A. tanguticum*.

P.K. Very long-lived in full sun or partial shade, *Allium karataviense* has a dramatic effect that can be overwhelming in a small place or otherworldly rising out of a carpet of veronica. *Allium moly* is aggressive and should be relegated to wild gardens or wild corners. *Allium cyaneum*, however, with its nodding cornflower blue clusters is an example of the many restrained dwarf onions that enliven late-summer gardens.

G.S. These two, as well as other species of onions including *Allium flavum* and *A. oreophilum*, are available and easy to grow. Avoid the tallest species, which are too large for most rock gardens. Our native *A. cernuum* and *A. acuminatum* are also good, if grown in a spot that dries out in summer.

Anemone spp

(anemone, windflower)

Anemones are members of the buttercup family and native to many parts of the north temperate zone. Among them are a number of tuberous or rhizomatous hardy species (more delicate versions of the large-flowered florists' anemones), which in size and habit are suited to the rock garden. Primarily woodland plants, they require well-drained, humus-rich sandy soil and some shade. Plant the tubers in early fall.

B.J. *Anemone blanda** has been grown in our area for many years. It is sometimes difficult to get started, however, because purchased tubers may have dried out too much. We have found the large-flowered variety 'Bridesmaid' extremely good. *Anemone nemorosa* grows very well for us in a woodsy soil in light shade, and *A. canadensis* is excellent provided it is kept in check. I have seen fine-looking *A. coronaria* in my area, but I have not grown it myself. Many anemones die down after flowering, so be careful not to dig them up unintentionally.

T.C. Most anemones grow best in a woodsy soil and partial shade. Especially suited to the rock garden are two European species, *Anemone nemorosa* (with white flowers) and *A. ranunculoides* (with yellow). Both are spring-flowering and grow from thin rhizomes. The Greek species *A. blanda* is often offered in bulb catalogues.

A.P. *Anemone apennina* has clear blue many-sepalled flowers, although mauve, pink and white variants exist; it is tuberous and grows to 6 inches. *Anemone nemorosa* is similar, typically white with purplish backs to the sepals, and double forms exist. Both these species flower April to May. *Anemone blanda* is more dwarf (3 inches) and earlier (early April), and its blossoms are typically purple-blue. This whole group is extremely valuable. Other species to consider: *A. narcissiflora*, apple-blossom anemone from the Alps, with sprays of white flowers in early summer, and *A. sylvestris*, which is like a miniature spring-flowering Japanese anemone.

P.K. This genus contains a great number of valuable rock garden plants. The tuberous *Anemone blanda* and *A. apen-* 69

*doxa luciliae** produces several starry blue flowers, paling to white centres, on each 4-to-6-inch stalk, amid fairly broad leaves that curve inward along the edges. There are also white and very pale pink forms. Although – like some other small bulbs – they are most effective in drifts or in sheets of colour, they are nonetheless charming in a rock garden setting where their detail may be appreciated. With a moderately fertile and well-drained soil, and left undisturbed, they will increase naturally through offsets and some self-seeding into a very pleasing little colony. Plant bulbs 2 or 3 inches apart in fall.

B.J. *Chionodoxa luciliae* has grown and prospered in Newfoundland for generations. More often used here beneath light deciduous shade, it is also nice and cheerful for the spring rock garden. Ideal for planting beneath miniature ground covers such as *Paronychia serpyllifolia*.

T.C. As its name suggests, this is one of the first spring flowers. It should be dug up and replanted every few years to keep the bulbs increasing. Grows best in well-drained soils.

nina tolerate ordinary rock garden culture, while *A. nemorosa* is long-lived and vigorous in woodland garden conditions. *Anemone sylvestris* can be a pest in most soils with its rapidly spreading rhizomes, but *A. magellanica* and *A. biarmiensis* provide similar flowers without spreading. There are many less frequently grown anemones that deserve to be tested and grown more widely.

G.S. A very useful genus of small plants growing from hard, irregular tubers. I like them in the garden because of their fernlike foliage, which is a pleasing contrast to the typical grasslike foliage of spring bulbs. Small bulbs look good pushing up through the anemone foliage. *Anemone blanda* and *A. nemorosa* are extremely common and tend to be invasive in the Vancouver area, but they are showy in the spring with their pale blue, pink or white flowers.

Chionodoxa luciliae

(glory-of-the-snow)

Chionodoxa is a hardy spring-flowering native of Crete and Asia Minor. *Chiono-*

A.P. Lovely and easy but possibly better for massing under shrubs than in a specialist rock garden.

P.K. Best displayed in large colonies of 50 to 100 plants. Seems to prefer fairly rich loam or some peat in our climate and not the hottest location. Its vibrant blue is especially nice contrasted with miniature daffodils or *Tulipa tarda*.

G.S. A good and easy little bulb grown commonly in our area. It is small enough to fit well in even the smallest of rock gardens. Bulbs are available from most bulb suppliers.

Claytonia virginica

(spring beauty)

A wildflower of the early spring woods, *Claytonia virginica** is common throughout the northeastern United States and eastern Canada. The narrow leaves are succulent, the flowers white streaked with pink. It requires a shady, moist location and therefore is useful only in a rock garden that can supply these needs. If you are able to establish a small colony of the corms in a spot that is to their liking, they will spread and increase on their own.

B.J. More suited to a damp, shaded corner of the woodland bed. An unusual native in Newfoundland.

T.C. I have never tried this woodlander in the rock garden. It should thrive in a shady area.

A.P. Charming native for half shade.

P.K. Not cultivated in this area. The similar *Claytonia lanceolata* fills the ponderosa pine woodlands of our foothills, but we have never seen it in either garden or nursery. *Claytonia megarhiza* is a glorious alpine plant that can be cultivated with care in a cool scree.

G.S. I have not seen this species in any Vancouver garden, although it should grow here.

Corydalis spp

(fumitory)

Another genus of the north temperate zone, *Corydalis* has annual and biennial species, as well as herbaceous perennials with rhizomatous roots and tubers. The foliage is graceful and fernlike, the flowers reminiscent of bleeding heart.

Corydalis solida (syn. *C. bulbosa*), one of the tuberous perennials, produces pinkish and occasionally white flowers early in spring, and thereafter the foliage dies down completely – this is the best time to transplant. All prefer light shade and moist but well-drained soil with plenty of organic matter. Tubers will split and form new plants as they age.

T.C. This tiny bulb deserves more attention. It has proved to be very hardy (surviving minus 39 degrees F) and is multiplying slowly. The pale mauve flowers appear in early spring, and the entire plant has finished its growth cycle and become dormant in a few weeks. It requires a well-drained soil; clay would probably prove fatal.

A.P. *Corydalis solida* is a pleasant little 71

pink-flowered spring species. *Corydalis cachmeriana* blooms a wonderful gentian blue in summer.

P.K. Its flowers a rather dingy, purplish hue, *Corydalis solida* bursts into growth, flowers and vanishes into dormancy as quickly as its American cousin *Dicentra cucullaria*. In a cool, shady spot, it will spread with great abandon both by seed and vegetatively, yet it is still welcome in all but the smallest gardens.

G.S. The *Corydalis* species are generally not very common here, but several are grown by specialists. *Corydalis cheilanthifolia** is especially attractive because of its ferny, coppery and pale green foliage, as well as its yellow flowers.

Crocus spp

(crocus)

Members of the iris family, crocuses are among the most popular and best-known spring flowers. Here it is necessary to distinguish between the slender "wild," or "species," crocuses and the larger, more opulent "Dutch" crocuses of the full-colour catalogues. Most of the species crocuses bloom earlier than their horticultural cousins, especially if they are

tucked into a sheltered corner of the rock garden away from spring winds, and they remain in bloom longer. If you include autumn-flowering crocuses in your collection, you greatly increase the time span during which these plants may be enjoyed. Plant the corms (thick bulblike stem bases) quite early in September, where they may self-sow freely.

B.J. Crocuses are out of my field at present. However, one of our local enthusiasts advises me that he successfully grows the following: *Crocus nudiflorus, C. speciosus* and *C. × pulchellus*, all autumn crocuses. For spring blooms, he grows *C. ancyrensis, C. vernus, C. tomasinianus, C. corsicus, C. minimus* and at least seven varieties of *C. chrysanthus.**

T.C. The spring-flowering crocuses need little comment; to most people, they *are* the flowers of spring. First to flower of the commonly available forms is a bright yellow species crocus, *Crocus ancyrensis*, and some named clones of *C. chrysanthus* such as 'Snow Bunting.' In addition to the common spring crocus, there are a number of species that flower in the fall. The best known of these is the source of saffron, *C. sativus*. This has not proved to be hardy in Ottawa. From a collection of a dozen or so species planted one fall, most bloomed but only two produced leaves the following spring, and those never flowered again.

A.P. Some spring species that I would recommend include *Crocus vernus, C. chrysanthus, C. tomasinianus, C. susianus*; among the autumn species are *C. speciosus, C. zonatus*. All are splendid except *C. sativus*, which produces saffron but tends to flower erratically.

P.K. This genus performs to perfection in the sunny springs of the Rocky Mountain region. Bulbs rapidly form large clumps and even spread by seed in any gravelly, loamy or peaty soil, thriving in sun or partial shade. The widely available hybrids and selections of *Crocus vernus* are too large and fleshy to be at home amongst the wildflowers of the rock garden, but the wild ancestor of these hybrids (*C. vernus albiflorus*) will grow well on a cool bank. The real glory for us is *C. chrysanthus* in its many forms, which are cheaply and easily available. Should be grown by the hundreds for the long spring season. *Crocus sativus* survives and occasionally sends up one glorious flower in fall. Its culture has not been mastered here. *Crocus speciosus* and the similar *C. pulchellus* do best in a soil that contains some peat and is not bone-dry. They begin to bloom here in October and often last well into November.

G.S. Crocuses are the only small bulbs grown by almost all gardeners. Many of the spring-flowering species are readily available and easy to grow, multiplying over the years with no care. The autumn-flowering species are not seen as often, but I personally like these the best, as they flower at a time when we have very few bulbs in bloom. Unfortunately, autumn rains often beat down the flowers. Many species are grown only in botanical gardens and by alpine plant and bulb enthusiasts.

Cyclamen hederifolium; C. europeum

(hardy cyclamen)

The rock garden cyclamens, members of the primula family, are miniature versions of the larger, better-known florists' species, *Cyclamen persicum*. *Cyclamen europeum* (syn. *C. purpurascens*), a native of the Swiss Alps, has the same familiar heart-shaped, mottled leaves – several sizes smaller with rosy blossoms – and is considered hardy in the northern United States; *C. hederifolium* * (syn. *C. neapolitanum*), its leaves silver-patterned and flowers red or white, is hardy in the northeast. Give them leaf mould and lime and a lightly shaded place where the tubers will be undisturbed.

B.J. We still have a lot to learn about the potential of these plants in Newfoundland. *Cyclamen hederifolium* thrives in our woodland bed in close companionship with *Erythronium americanum*. *Cyclamen coum*, *C. c. caucasicum* and *C. purpurascens* are also showing promise for us in our general area.

73

T.C. I have never had the nerve to try this outside over winter. It is a native of the Mediterranean area, and I doubt if it would be hardy here.

A.P. With its autumn flowers, *Cyclamen hederifolium* is the best species for general use. Seems pretty hardy in spite of overwintering leaves. *Cyclamen coum* and *C. repandum* should also be mentioned. Grow in limy soil; can take half shade.

P.K. *Cyclamen hederifolium* seems to be the only cyclamen that will thrive in Colorado. It wants a soil containing leaf mould and the cover of a light, loose mulch of leaves and does best in the shade of deciduous trees. Often starts blooming in August.

G.S. This species and several others, particularly *Cyclamen coum* and *C. repandum*, are very showy and choice alpine plants, flowering in autumn, mild winters or spring, depending on the species. The heart-shaped, mottled foliage is a pleasing texture in the garden, even when the plants are not in flower. A number of species and forms are commonly available here and widely grown. Easy to raise and care-free, they prefer light shade but tolerate full sun in our climate. These small species are much more refined and attractive than the florists' large *C. persicum*.

Eranthis hyemalis

(winter aconite)

In northern regions, winter aconite is often the first bulb to appear, even ahead of the snowdrop. Its miniature blossoms, like marsh marigolds, surrounded by a ruff of dark green leaves, reach no higher than 2 or 3 inches. *Eranthis hyemalis** can thrive in any good well-drained garden soil and appreciates some shade. If left undisturbed, it will self-seed and increase. It is important to plant the tubers as early as possible, in early September or even August, as growth begins at that time.

74   B.J. Will grow very well in some

gardens but not in others. Susceptible to frost damage, so a good and lasting snow cover is indicated. It is reputed to have naturalized here, but generally speaking, I doubt that this happens in many sites.

T.C. This is another of the spring-flowering bulbs that I would not be without. I read that the trick to success with these is to soak the bulbs for 24 hours before you plant. This certainly turns them from little pieces of dried-up leather into something more like a bulb, but the one time I tried this, I had the worst results ever. (It probably didn't help that a dog had buried its bone in that spot.) The native habitat of winter aconites is at the edge of a woods, the kind of place where trilliums grow, so a shady, humus-rich site is best for them.

A.P. Can naturalize in large swathes, but half a dozen plants sheltered beneath a rock garden shrub are just as welcome. *Eranthis* × *tubergenii* is a more robust hybrid.

P.K. The shrivelled tubers usually

available by mail order or from local nurseries may or may not revive if soaked overnight in warm water and planted in partial shade. Try to find someone from whom to obtain divisions or seedlings in the spring. Once established, it spreads gleefully in cool exposures.

G.S. A nice little tuberous plant, usually sold in the autumn with the true bulbs. It flowers very early, with relatively large yellow "buttercups" held above a ring of dissected leaves. It is generally not very long-lived in the Vancouver area but worth growing even if it has to be renewed every year.

Fritillaria meleagris

(chequered lily, fritillary)

Members of the lily family, fritillaries are found throughout the temperate zones of the world, but of the 70 or so species that exist, only a few are cultivated. The guinea hen flower, chequered lily or snake's head fritillary, *Fritillaria meleagris,** is one of them and is an intriguing early-blooming presence in the rock garden with its purplish, veined, bell-like blossoms and delicate, slender leaves. There are also white- and yellow-flowered forms. Plant the bulbs early in the fall; every two or three years thereafter, they may be divided and increased by offsets.

B.J. More suited to rich organic soil in the light shade of a woodland bed, where it will put on a most interesting display. Many rock gardens would be too dry and exposed for this plant.

T.C. This delicate plant thrives in a slightly shaded site with a soil high in humus. It has established itself and spread slowly in Ottawa. Plant the white form in deeper shade where its colour will shine, and the dull pink form (with its network of chocolate veins that gives this its common names) toward the front in brighter light.

A.P. A plant of moist, limy meadows but happy in most sites. Lovely, dis-

tinctive bells, purple or white.

P.K. Easily grown and long-lived in any partly shaded rockwork with a gritty, humusy soil.

G.S. This is a very large genus of bulbs, many of which are small enough for the rock garden. *Fritillaria meleagris* is the species most often available and one of the most charming, with its drooping bells of purplish brown or white. It is one of my favourite spring bulbs, although many other species are grown by bulb enthusiasts.

Galanthus nivalis

(snowdrop)

A native of Europe and southwest Asia, *Galanthus nivalis** is one of the early comers in spring, despite snow and cold. It is a small, hardy bulbous plant much ap-   75 preciated for its delicacy and understated elegance. The solitary, nodding white blooms with touches of green at the edges stand barely 4 inches high, with two or three narrow leaves to accompany them. Though they are splendid massed in a woodland setting, they are also quite at home clustered in the corners of a rock garden where they can enjoy the cool, moist humusy soil they need. Bulbs should be planted early, in August if possible, and if left undisturbed, they will form well-established colonies.

B.J. Has thrived in Newfoundland for well over a century. Can be used in the rock garden but is better suited to a naturalistic woodland setting.

T.C. Another of the very early spring flowers that will often push its way up through the snow to bloom. Old gardening books from the turn of the century list dozens of forms of snowdrop, but now all we seem to get are single and double ones. Personally, I never consider the double form worth the extra price. Unless you are going to lie on the cold wet ground to peer inside the bell, you do not notice any difference.

A.P. All snowdrops are good. *Galanthus nivalis* is more usual in quantity under shrubs or in woodland. Other eastern European species – *G. elwesii* and *G. plicatus*, for instance – need more care and, hence, rock garden spots. Limy soil preferred. It is convenient but not mandatory to divide established clumps directly after flowering.

P.K. Blooms for several months as spring and winter battle for supremacy. Likes cool temperatures and some humus. *Galanthus elwesii* has broader leaves and seems to tolerate a little more sun. These are both outstanding plants that will naturalize in Rocky Mountain gardens.

G.S. A genus of very easy, very commonly grown spring bulbs. Depending on the winter, they may begin flowering at any time from December to February and continue for several weeks. They are not showy but are easy to grow and valuable, if for no other reason than to give the feeling that spring has arrived.

Iris spp

(dwarf iris)

Irises have been treasured for centuries as being among the most beautiful of plants; in more recent years, hybridization has produced many new, vigorous varieties in exquisite colours and forms, which are gradually replacing the older types. However, for rock garden culture, spectacular size and colour are out of place, and it is from the many dwarf species available that the gardener should make a selection. The irises are a complex tribe divided into groups according to their root characteristics (bulbous, rhizomatous or fibrous) and their flower forms (bearded, beardless); these groups are further divided into subgroups.

Leaving aside such complications, any dwarf species may be considered for the rock garden, no matter what its category, provided care is taken to understand and meet its particular needs. *Iris reticulata*, a bulbous species ("wild") plant comprising a number of varieties, blooms in early spring with fragrant single blossoms in the blue-violet range, only a few inches high. It looks very effective planted with a low-growing, early perennial such as arabis and likes a neutral, well-drained soil in a sunny location. The bulbs must be planted 6 to 8 inches deep. *Iris cristata*,* 6 to 9 inches tall, blooms in late spring with multitudes of blue, gold-crested flowers; its matted, rhizomatous root system requires a woodsy soil and some shade. Among bearded irises (look for the "beard" on the lower petals of the flowers) is *I. pumila*, early-blooming and nearly stemless, from Austria and Asia Minor in the wild, but also much hybridized and therefore available in a great range of colours. They need good drainage and much sun, and their shallow rhizomes benefit from being divided and replanted every three years or so.

B.J. Some smaller irises have potential in the rock garden here in Newfoundland. *Iris pumila*, *I. cristata*, *I. graminea* and the native *I. setosa* (syn. *I. hookeri*) grow well for us once they have settled down. Some difficulty is experienced with frost heave, but a mulch of washed small gravel helps to anchor the roots without rotting them.

T.C. The bulbous irises, such as *Iris reticulata* and *I. danfordiae*, are some of the first flowers to appear in the spring. Like snowdrops, they often push through the last of the snow. Although they have never naturalized in Ottawa (and have had to be replanted every few years), I would not consider it spring without them.

A.P. *All* are valuable.

P.K. *Iris danfordiae* and *I. reticulata* are wonderful and durable in good loams, and

many of these plants actually increase rapidly over the years. *Iris pumila*, in its hundreds of forms and hybrids, is both heat- and drought-tolerant and pest-free as well. *Iris cristata*, on the other hand, requires moist shade, and the flowers seldom last for more than a week. This is an ideal climate for virtually any iris; even the Pacific Coast iris can be grown with just a little shade.

G.S. These are all excellent plants for the rock garden. The bulbous ones are among the earliest to bloom and are readily available and inexpensive. *Iris reticulata* is long-lived here and forms large clumps after a few years if grown in a very sunny, well-drained situation; it gives a splash of royal blue or purple to the garden. *Iris danfordiae* is showy but usually doesn't survive more than a year or two. Both are well liked by slugs. The dwarf bearded iris cultivars of *I. pumila* are fairly common here and are relatively easy. *Iris cristata* is a nice little iris forming large clumps. There are several species of West Coast native irises (*I. innominata*, *I. bracteata*, *I. douglasiana* and *I. chrysophylla*) and their Pacific hybrids that are grown in our area and are very choice. *Iris unguicularis*   77 is also considered very desirable for our area because of its winter flowers.

Muscari botryoides; M. azureum

(grape hyacinth)

Grape hyacinths are members of the lily family that originated in the Mediterranean region. *Muscari botryoides** is the more commonly grown and familiar species; *M. azureum*, a native of Turkey, does not differ greatly from it in appearance, both being small bulbous plants possessing the characteristic blue spire-like flower heads on 6-inch stems. One must look closely to see that the individual flowers of *M. azureum* are more open and more nearly bell-shaped than those of *M. botryoides*. The great difference between the two species lies in their habits: *M. botryoides* is aggressive, with sprawling, untidy leaves, while *M. azureum* is more self-effacing and neater and therefore to be preferred in the rock garden setting. All grape hyacinths seem to prefer sun and a rich but somewhat sandy soil. Plant bulbs in September or early October; once in the ground, they need little attention. Propagation is by seeds and offsets.

B.J. While I am not familiar with *Muscari azureum* in Newfoundland, *M. botryoides* and its white form *M.b. album* grow well in the St. John's area. *Muscari armeniacum* may be the more common and hardy species here.

T.C. Both the blue and the white forms of *Muscari botryoides* do well. I prefer the Armenian grape hyacinth (*M. armeniacum*) – especially the cultivar 'Blue Spike' with its noteworthy double flowers.

A.P. *Muscari botryoides* puts on a good spring show, but its leaves begin to grow in the fall and can flop over choicer things. A Turkish native, *M. azureum* is an excellent little grape hyacinth without the untidy leaves of its cousin.

P.K. An aggressive plant, *Muscari botryoides* produces evergreen (and seldom pretty) leaves that persist virtually year-round and detract greatly from its usefulness. The white form is widely available and seems to be less invasive. *Muscari azureum* is a trim miniature with all the charm and none of the faults of its relative. Its short chubby leaves appear in early spring with Cambridge-blue flowers and gracefully withdraw soon afterward. In a few years, a single bulb will form a colourful patch. This species also has an excellent white form. It tolerates sun or partial shade in any good garden loam. Other useful muscari species include *M.* 'Plumosa,' which is a dramatic, showy plant, and the similar *M.* 'Comosa' with its shaggy flower heads; both are striking and determined to spread. *Muscari tubergenianum*, with its lovely baby-blue flowers in mid-spring, is both charming and restrained.

G.S. *Muscari botryoides* is one of our most commonly grown bulbs, tiny enough to fit into even the smallest rock garden,

78

very easy and long-lasting. I am not really familiar with *M. azureum.*

Narcissus spp

(dwarf daffodils)

The narcissus family of hardy bulbous plants, mostly of European origin, represents to many people the ultimate in spring flowers because of the fragrance and the clear whites, oranges and yellows, whether in the form of daffodils, jonquils, paperwhites or their many hybridized varieties. They are classified according to flower types, but the rock gardener is less concerned with these intricacies than with choosing from amongst the extroverted array those which in size and temperament will be in tune with the other inhabitants of the rock garden. There are many delicate, dwarf species daffodils that fill these requirements admirably; they and their own hybrids have a natural affinity for rocks, and though they can hold their own amidst other rock garden plants and ground covers, they will not increase so rapidly as to need frequent replanting. Some of the best are *Narcissus bulbocodium* (hoop petticoat), *N. triandrus** and *N. asturiensis.* They all appreciate a well-drained, sandy loam. Old clumps may be lifted and divided after the foliage has completely died down; new bulbs should be planted as early in the fall as possible, so that new roots can grow before freeze-up.

B.J. Our local rock gardeners have done very little with this particular plant group. There are many kinds to try, and provided they are not of the type that require very hot, dry summers, it would be worth growing any that come your way. Some that are showing promise here are *Narcissus asturiensis* (sold as *N. minimus*), *N. nanus*, *N. juncifolius*, *N. triandrus* hybrids and *N. cyclamineus* 'Tête-à-Tête.'

T.C. There are a great number of miniature narcissus, both species and hybrids, suitable for the rock garden. I have had success with *Narcissus minor* and *N. bulbocodium*, but *N. watieri* did not survive long. The hybrids are much longer-lasting; a planting of *N. cyclamineus* 'Peeping Tom' survived almost 20 years until it was killed off by an unusually cold winter. Narcissus do not seem to take much below minus 25 degrees F. I would particularly recommend 'Tête-à-Tête,' 'March Sunshine,' the double 'Rip van Winkle' and, for larger gardens, *N. triandrus* hybrids such as 'Thalia.'

A.P. *Narcissus bulbocodium, N. triandrus, N. cyclamineus* (in moister soil) and their hybrids are always a joy. Every small narcissus can be recommended.

P.K. All seem to appreciate extra moisture and some shade. Many cultivars are available in rock garden sizes, and *Narcissus asturiensis* is especially nice among the species narcissus.

G.S. The small and often quite showy 79

species narcissus extend the spring-bulb season over many months. The first and one of the smallest often grown here – but not well enough known – is *Narcissus asturiensis* (*N. minimus*), which usually begins to bloom in January. Slightly larger and later are *N. minor*, *N. rupicola* and *N. triandrus*, as well as *N. cyclamineus*, which is long-lasting in terms of flowering time and permanence in the garden. A few small hybrids are 'February Gold,' 'February Silver' and 'Tête-à-Tête.' A number of other species are seen in bulb specialists' gardens.

Puschkinia scilloides

(striped squill)

This spring bloomer is an attractive but not very showy member of the lily family and closely related to scilla. The pale blue,

striped bell-like blossoms, clustered on 4- to-6-inch stems, look well if planted in close colonies with mat-forming plants such as pink iberis. *Puschkinia scilloides libanotica** has somewhat longer petals. The bulbs are hardy and should be planted in September or early October, in a nutrient-rich soil in sun or partial shade. After a number of years, if flowering declines, they may be dug up when the foliage has fully ripened. Detach bulblets and replant in fresh soil.

B.J. Have been raised successfully in Newfoundland for years.

T.C. Grow this for its scent, if for no other reason. It is similar to the better-known scilla, but will bring you fragrance in the spring.

A.P. Different, but less effective than either chionodoxa or scilla.

P.K. In sunny loam or partial shade, this squill can self-sow with abandon. A very colourful bulb, useful when separated from less extroverted plants.

G.S. A commonly grown bulb in the Vancouver area. The pale blue flowers need a dark background, such as a very low ground cover, for their best show. Otherwise, they may be lost against light-coloured soils.

Scilla sibirica

(Siberian squill, spring squill)

This is the earliest of the squills to bloom. *Scilla sibirica*,* its brilliant blue bell-shaped flowers rising from a grasslike cluster of leaves, is easy to grow and increases rapidly. Since it will thrive in partial shade, it is especially useful in spring beneath shrubs and trees. However, it can be very effective in small colonies in the rock garden, given the rich sandy soil with some shade that scillas prefer. Plant the bulbs September to October, and increase by bulblets taken from older bulbs in fall.

B.J. A very popular spring bulb in Newfoundland but more often seen growing in masses beneath deciduous trees than in our local rock gardens.

T.C. Next to crocuses, these are probably the most widely grown rock garden bulbs. The pale blue flowers must be rich in nectar, since bees seem to find them on days when I would never expect to see bees foraging.

A.P. Makes a magnificent blue carpet under trees, even in shade. Often does better in North America than in Europe.

P.K. A glorious blue companion plant to tulips and daffodils, it does best here with a little shade.

G.S. One of my favourite little spring bulbs. The intense blue flowers of large size on small plants are perfect for the rock garden. They are widely available, easy to grow and long-lasting.

Tulipa spp

Tulips have a long and romantic history dating from the time when the Turks, the first to become interested in developing them from the wild, overran parts of southern Europe and brought tulip cultivation with them. The variety of sizes, types and colours can be bewildering, but the rock gardener may once more cut a delicate swathe through to the smaller species plants, which in themselves offer quite a scope in terms of blossom shape and colour. Many of them keep their slender, pointed blooms closed morning and evening and on cloudy days but open them into wide flat stars when the sun is out. While they bloom early in spring on the whole, they continue to bloom longer than their more showy relatives elsewhere in the garden. Some of the species, such as *Tulipa kaufmanniana* and *T. dasystemon*, may self-seed and form colonies in ideal situations, but they do not naturalize as freely as some of the daffodils and are more fussy about their environment. They need a sandy soil, particularly good drainage and hot sun during the summer; the rock garden may provide an excellent site. Tulip bulbs may be planted later in the fall than most other bulbs, provided they go in before the ground freezes. Many people choose to plant them quite deeply (8 to 10 inches), which lessens the danger of botrytis and the depredations of squirrels and other animal pests.

B.J. To grow consistently well, tulips require dry, hot summers, and so Newfoundland is not the greatest place on earth for them. *Tulipa kaufmanniana* grows here but may be too large for the average rock garden until it has bloomed a couple of times. *Tulipa tarda** (*T. dasystemon*) is most desirable and performs well, while *T. urumiensis* is also worth a trial.

T.C. As with narcissus, there are numerous species and hybrid tulips that deserve a place in the rock garden. In fact, a rock garden without tulips would be hard to imagine. *Tulipa tarda* is probably about the most reliable and will seed itself and pop up in all sorts of places. This and

81

T. urumiensis, from Iran, have yellow flowers. Red-flowered *T. linifolia* and *T. maximowiczii* also survive well in this climate. Try, too, the pale lilac-coloured *T. pulchella*. Best of all the species-related tulips are the various hybrids of *T. greigii* and *T. kaufmanniana*. *Tulipa greigii* is attractive even when not in flower, since its leaves are mottled with chocolate-coloured veins. Many of the named forms, such as 'Red Riding Hood,' grow only 8 inches tall; the waterlily tulip, *T. kaufmanniana*, has many low-growing forms from 4 to 12 inches in height.

A.P. *All* dwarf tulip species are to be recommended fully, but some of the newer *Tulipa kaufmanniana, greigii* and *fosteriana* hybrids are too big and bright for most rock garden scenes. Plant all at least 6 to 8 inches deep, and do not lift annually unless "tulip fire" (*Botrytis tulipae*) becomes a curse.

P.K. Virtually all the species tulips are long-lived and vigorous in sunny rock gardens here, and they seem to appreciate the baking summer heat. Perhaps the showiest are *Tulipa humilis, T. batalinii* and *T. linifolia*, while the dozens of cultivars of *T. kaufmanniana* and *T. greigii* are suitable for larger gardens.

G.S. Most *Tulipa* species are not long-lasting in our area and are best bought and replaced each fall. They are easy and showy the first year, however, and some of the species do come back for a few years. The large hybrids are all too big for the rock garden, but the species *T. kaufmanniana, T. praestans, T. batalinii, T. tarda, T. clusiana* and *T. turkestanica* are all small enough to fit well in rock gardens and are all grown in our area.

Zephyranthes spp

(zephyr-lily, fairy-lily, rain-lily)

These small lilylike members of the amaryllis family are natives of southern areas of the western hemisphere – South America, Mexico, Cuba, southeastern United States – and, as such, are generally not hardy north of Washington, D.C. Because of this, they may be treated as other tender bulbs: planted in spring in a sandy soil with good humus content, lifted before the frost comes and stored indoors over winter in a medium such as peat moss, which reduces air circulation. Some species are early-blooming, and others such as *Zephyranthes candida*,* put out their flowers in late summer or fall. Their attractive solitary flowers on 6-to-8-inch stalks range in colour from white and pink to bright yellow and copper; the leaves are slender and grasslike. The bulbs are readily available from many bulb suppliers, and they might be worth at least one trial in the rock garden – if only to satisfy an alphabetical whim.

B.J. I know nobody who has grown this plant, and I don't think it would survive here outside.

T.C. I have not actually grown these in Ottawa but can see no reason why they should not thrive if treated like gladiolus and dug up each fall. They may well survive with a heavy mulch of leaves in the fall once the ground has frozen.

A.P. *Zephyranthes candida* – like a white autumn crocus with grassy, almost evergreen, leaves. I doubt if it would take winters here, and it does not dry off enough to lift out and store. This species would probably work well with others such as *Z. rosea* for a late-summer display.

P.K. No species of zephyranthes has thus far proved to be reliably hardy in Colorado.

G.S. Known as rain-lilies since, where they are native, the flowers appear when the cooler days and autumn rains begin. The delicate pink or white flowers are attractive in the fall, but they are not seen in our area very often, except in botanical gardens or as cool greenhouse plants. Although they should be hardy here, too much winter rain makes them short-lived. If given a sunny, very well-drained location, they survive for a few years. Certain kinds are usually available where spring-flowering bulbs are sold, and they should be grown more often than they are.

More Options

While the herbaceous perennials and some carefully chosen bulbs may be the mainstays of the rock garden, a few other plant forms have a definite place, texturally and visually, among them.

Ferns

Many ferns are native to sunny, rocky areas and so go well in this environment, where their foliage contrasts gracefully with other plants. For a shady rock garden, there are ferns that grow well in a woodsy soil and can be planted between bulbs and wildflowers so that their fronds are expanding as the flowers and foliage of the other plants fade. They can also be planted under nearby trees and shrubs to soften the transition between these and the rock garden. Avoid invasive ferns with spreading roots such as the hay-scented fern, the lady fern, the sensitive fern and bracken. Ferns for sun include: *Ceterach officinarum, Cryptogramma crispa, Cheilanthes gracillima*; for shade: *Adiantum pedatum*, small species of *Asplenium, Blechnum, Dryopteris* and *Woodsia* and *Athrium goeringianum pictum*.

Grasses

Many plants grow among grasses in the wild, and in fact, there are probably more grasses, sedges and rushes in the mountains than there are flowering plants. A number of the clumping types look well in the rock garden, where their tufts of green and grey can be very restful. The airy stems of other types may lighten nearby plantings. Most like sun, though a few are shade-lovers. Avoid any that are described as stoloniferous, or spreading. A few good grasses, all of which will eventually need division, are *Carex* 83 *morrowi variegata*, *Festuca ovina* 'Glauca' and *Arrhenatherum elatius* 'Variegatum.'

Annuals

Annuals for the rock garden should be low and have the character of rock garden plants, with tidy compact growth; they should look like a species and not a full-blown border plant. These can be useful in several ways: to cover bare places created when bulb foliage disappears or when a plant dies; to soften newly constructed areas; and to give colour late in the season. Three attractive small annuals are *Ionopsidium acaule* (diamond flower), *Dyssodia tenuiloba* (Dahlberg daisy) and *Sanvitalia procumbens* (creeping zinnia). There are some genuine alpine annuals, such as *Androsace lactiflora*, *A. septentrionalis* and *Saxifraga cymbalaria*, that often self-sow and come up each year.

Dwarf Shrubs and Conifers

Finally, all our contributors agreed on the importance of dwarf shrubs and conifers, plants that never attain the size of the species from which they were derived. Planned for, if not incorporated, right from the beginning, they give weight, permanence and "backbone" to the garden, provide contrasting heights and textures and add winter interest. They should be treated as part of the overall design, accenting and complementing both rocks and low-growing plants.

It is important, therefore, when looking first of all at shrubs, to know the ultimate height and spread in order to gauge their compatibility with other plants; many so-called dwarfs often grow too large too soon. Dwarf hollies (*Ilex* spp), boxwoods (*Buxus* spp) and daphnes (*Daphne* spp) may be useful, as well as some small willows (*Salix* spp), brooms (*Genista* spp) and spireas (*Spiraea* spp). Some of the best, most ornamental plants are the ericaceous shrubs – heaths, heathers, rhododendrons, azaleas and other related species – found all over the world in cool temperate zones and in mountainous parts of the tropics. Most are evergreen, so they are attractive in the garden year-round. Numerous dwarf forms combine well with other acid-loving plants such as gentians, primroses and small wildflowers. Their soil should be an acid, peaty, sandy mixture that does not dry out, and most will need some protection from winter sun and wind and a certain amount of shade in summer. If your rock garden can provide these conditions, you will have a wealth of fine shrubs to choose from.

Many dwarf conifers originate from seed, some have been propagated from "witches' brooms" (abnormal bushlike growth on cedars and other plants) or other mutant forms, and others are stunted due to their environment; under normal conditions, the latter lose their dwarf habit. The solid feel of these little trees is similar to that of the rocks, and the greens, bronzes and golds of their foliage in winter are strong factors in their favour. Some can be too slow-growing, however, while others turn out not to be dwarf at all – a tiny 4-inch bun can become a 24-inch monster in no time. Careful pruning may keep the situation in check, but sometimes the tree simply has to be removed. Because of this, some gardeners prefer to use dwarf conifers near, rather than in, the rock garden. Nonetheless, if they can be incorporated successfully (one way or another) and prove to be sufficiently slow-growing to give several years' interest and beauty to your rock garden scene, they are well worth experimenting with. Before deciding on a plant for your particular site, read whatever you can find about it, and try to see it growing in a local garden or arboretum. There is a wealth of interesting dwarf species among *Juniperus* (juniper), *Chamaecyparis* (false cypress), *Abies* (fir), *Picea* (spruce), *Tsuga* (hemlock) and *Pinus* (pine).

CLIMATIC ZONE MAPS – CANADA

Lower zone numbers refer to increasingly cold areas, but there are not specific minimum temperature limits for each zone.

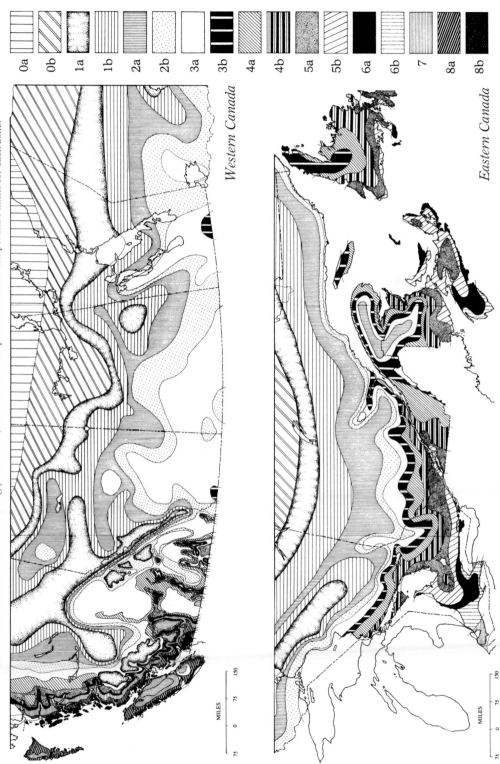

0a
0b
1a
1b
2a
2b
3a
3b
4a
4b
5a
5b
6a
6b
7
8a
8b

Western Canada

Eastern Canada

MILES
75 0 75 150

MILES
75 0 75 150

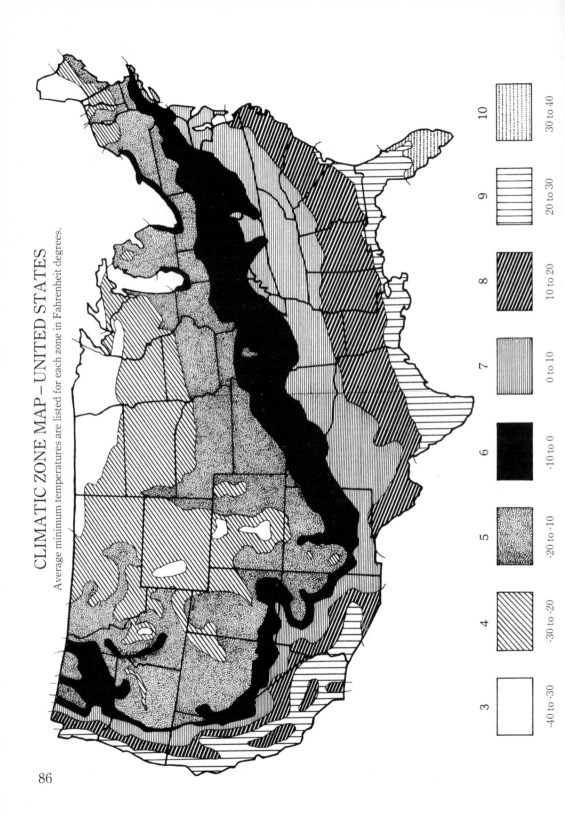

CLIMATIC ZONE MAP – UNITED STATES

Average minimum temperatures are listed for each zone in Fahrenheit degrees.

Zone	Temperature
3	-40 to -30
4	-30 to -20
5	-20 to -10
6	-10 to 0
7	0 to 10
8	10 to 20
9	20 to 30
10	30 to 40

Resources:
Rock Garden Societies and Publications

Rock Garden Societies

Ontario Rock Garden Society
c/o Andrew Osyany
Box 146
Shelburne, Ontario L0N 1S0
Membership $10; 10 issues of the
O.R.G.S. Journal annually, seed
exchanges, etc.

Alpine Garden Club of B.C.
c/o Denys Lloyd
Membership Chairman
3281 W. 35th Avenue
Vancouver, British Columbia
V6N 2M9
Membership $13; 5 bulletins annually.

**Vancouver Island Rock and
Alpine Garden Society**
c/o E.M. Browning
Box 6507, Postal Station C

Victoria, British Columbia
V8P 5M4
Local memberships only, please.

American Rock Garden Society
c/o Buffy Parker
15 Fairmead Road
Darien, Connecticut 06820
Membership $20 (U.S.); quarterly
bulletin, seed exchange, etc.

The Alpine Garden Society
c/o E.M. Upward, Secretary
Lye End Link, St. John's
Woking, Surrey GU21 ISW
England
Membership £12; quarterly bulletin
and twice yearly issue of *Alpine
Gardening*, seed distribution, etc.

The Scottish Rock Garden Club
c/o Miss K.M. Gibb

21 Merchiston Park
Edinburgh EH10 4PW
Scotland
Membership per year: send £5
international money order or $12 (U.S.).

Recommended Books

Rock Gardening: A Guide to Growing Alpines and Other Wildflowers in the American Garden by H. Lincoln Foster and Laura L. Foster (Houghton Mifflin Co.; Boston, 1968). More recent editions are also available.

How to Plan, Establish, and Maintain Rock Gardens by George H. Schenk (Lane Book Co.; Menlo Park, Calif., 1964). Sunset Books.

Rock Garden Plants by Doretta Klaber (Henry Holt; New York, 1959).

All About Rock Gardens and Plants by W.A. Kolaga (Doubleday and Co.; New York, 1966).

In a time of heightened conservation awareness, most people understand the concern over digging plants from the wild and appreciate the responsibility of the individual in protecting natural habitats. However, while one would choose to observe plants on their home ground, even the most rare are becoming increasingly accessible as nursery stock or seeds.

Mail order within one's own country presents few problems, and plants packed by a professional travel safely. Nor is there any problem with seeds ordered across an international border. For bulbs or any rooted plants, however, Canadians wishing to buy from U.S. or British nurseries that accept foreign orders should obtain an "application form for permit to import" from: The Permit Office, Plant Health Division, Agriculture Canada, Ottawa,

Ontario K1A 0C6. Request one application for each company from which you will order plants.

Imports to the U.S. must include an invoice showing the quantity and value of the plants, plus a document from the Department of Agriculture certifying that plants are disease-free.

Perennials, Seeds, Bulbs

All the well-known seed houses and nurseries offer a number of plants suitable for the rock garden, but a much greater selection is available from specialist nurseries.

Canada

Alpenflora Gardens
17985 40th Avenue
Surrey, British Columbia V3S 4N8

Many rock garden perennials, alpines. Catalogue under revision.

Honeywood Lilies & Nursery
Box 63
Parkside, Saskatchewan S0J 2A0
Specialists in lilies, including some species and low-growing hybrids. Lily catalogue $1.

McMillen's Iris Garden
RR 1
Norwich, Ontario N0J 1P0
A great variety of dwarf irises. Catalogue $1.

Stirling Perennials
RR 1
Morpeth, Ontario N0P 1X0
Hardy perennials, many alpines. Catalogue $1.

Tansy Farms
RR 1
5888 Else Road
Agassiz, British Columbia V0M 1A0
Herb specialists but also offer many plants for the rock garden. Catalogue $1.50.

Wrightman Alpine Plant Nursery
RR 3
Kerwood, Ontario N0M 2B0
Many rock garden perennials. Catalogue 50¢, to Canada only.

United States

Colorado Alpines, Inc.
Box 2708
Avon, Colorado 81620
Plants. Catalogue $2 (U.S.), refundable with order.

The Cummins Garden
22 Robertsville Road
Marlboro, New Jersey 07746
Dwarf rhododendrons, deciduous azaleas, dwarf evergreens, companion plants. Catalogue $1 (U.S.), refundable with order.

Far North Gardens
Dept. AG
16785 Harrison
Livonia, Michigan 48154
Seeds of rare plants from every continent. Catalogue $2 (U.S.).

J.L. Hudson, Seedsman
Box 1058
Redwood City, California 94064
Seeds. Catalogue $1 (U.S.).

Maver Seed
Route 2, Box 265B
Asheville, North Carolina 28805
Seeds. Alpine list $1 (U.S.).

Plants of the Southwest
1812 Second Street
Santa Fe, New Mexico 87501
Mail-order seeds, plants at nursery. Catalogue $1.50 (U.S.).

Rakestraws Gardens
3094 S. Term Street
Burton, Michigan 48529
Alpines, perennials, sedums, dwarf conifers and shrubs. Catalogue $1 (U.S.).

Rocknoll Nursery
9210 U.S. 50
Hillsboro, Ohio 45133
Rock plants, sempervivums, native American plants, irises, shrubs, dwarf evergreens; seed list. Catalogue 44¢ (U.S.) in stamps.

Roslyn Nursery
Dept. G
211 Burrs Lane
Dix Hills, New York 11746
Dwarf rhododendrons, azaleas, evergreens; perennials. Catalogue $2 (U.S.).

Siskiyou Rare Plant Nursery
Dept. 61
2825 Cummings Road
Medford, Oregon 97501
Catalogue $1.50 (U.S.). Shipping in
U.S.A. only.

Southwestern Native Seeds
Box 50503
Tucson, Arizona 85703
Seeds only, of a wide variety of plants.
Catalogue $1 (U.S.).

Thompson and Morgan
Box 1308
Jackson, New Jersey 08527
Large seed selection. Catalogue free.

United Kingdom

Jim and Jenny Archibald
Sherborne, Dorset DT9 5LD
England
Seed list of their own collections from
Europe, Asia Minor and, most
recently, the Rocky Mountain region.
No cost for list.

Chiltern Seeds
Bortree Stile
Ulverston, Cumbria LA12 7PB
England
Large seed list: South Africa,
Australia, Himalayas. Informative and
interesting catalogue £2 airmail.

Jack Drake
Inshriach Alpine Plant Nursery
Aviemore, Inverness-shire PH22 1QS
Scotland

Seeds only for export, list available
on request.

Holden Clough Nursery
Holden
Bolton-by-Bowland
Clitheroe, Lancashire BB7 4PF
England
Alpines, primulas, hardy perennials,
shrubs and dwarf conifers. Catalogue
$2 (U.S.) and seed list. Orders
dispatched worldwide.

Potterton and Martin
Nettleton
Nr. Caistor, North Lincolnshire
LN7 GHX
England
Dwarf bulbs. Catalogue $1 (U.S.).

Ferns and Ornamental Grasses

Hortico, Inc.
RR 1
Waterdown, Ontario L0R 2H0
Price list free.

Dwarf Shrubs and Conifers

Woodland Nurseries
2151 Camilla
Mississauga, Ontario L5A 2K1

Vineland Nurseries
Box 98
Vineland, Ontario L0R 2E0

Oslach Nurseries
RR 1
Simcoe, Ontario N3Y 4J9

Index

Credits